4 Ap

2

Champions of Democracy

CHAMPIONS
OF DEMOCRACY

BY

JOSEPH COTTLER

BOSTON
LITTLE, BROWN, AND COMPANY
1938

PRINTED IN THE UNITED STATES OF AMERICA

436044

TO BETTY

Come my tan-faced children,
Follow well in order, get your weapons ready,
Have you your pistols? have you your sharp-edged axes?
   Pioneers! O pioneers!

   For we cannot tarry here,
We must march my darlings, we must bear the brunt of
      danger,
We, the youthful sinewy races, all the rest on us depend,
   Pioneers! O pioneers!

   Till with sound of trumpet,
Far, far off the daybreak call — hark! how loud and clear
      I hear it wind,
Swift! to the head of the army! — swift! spring to your
      places,
   Pioneers! O pioneers!

WALT WHITMAN

Contents

I

The Voice in the Wilderness

ROGER WILLIAMS

This book tells the stories of twelve Americans who loved their country. "Sweet and beautiful" — in the words of an old Roman maxim — it was for them to live and die by that love. Yet theirs was no blind emotion, but a clear and disturbing thing. They knew why they loved America. It was not for her size, nor for her wealth, nor for her crowds. Often they preferred to overlook these features, and like lovers with vision to embrace the Ideal. How that Ideal was revealed to them, and with what agony they struggled to uphold it — that is their story. It begins with the time when America was but a frontier of Europe.

THE VOICE IN THE WILDERNESS

I

LONG before dawn, shadows had been moving in the Indian trail and when the autumn sun rose on field and forest about Boston, it lit up no usual Thursday in the year 1635. The shadows took shape, turned into bonnets and capes, goodman and goodwife, bound for Newton Church. Servants, this one day, were left in charge of work; for the General Court of the Colony was sitting at Newton Church. As usual the Court would pass laws, punish crimes. But the excitement — which had been gathering for months, nay years, to be spent at last that eighth of October — had to do with Master Williams. Roger Williams, teacher and minister at Salem, was to be tried that day.

The way to the square wooden church led past the pillory, past the whipping post. Whatever Master Williams' crimes, they could not bring him to that. To be whipped and branded with hot irons, to have one's head and hands locked in the pillory — these were penalties paid by simple folk,

3

not by people of quality, like Roger Williams. For crimes not unlike his, Philip Ratcliff had been fined, whipped, had his ears cut off, and been banished. But he had been a servant. Master Williams' ears were safe.

As the hour of the official trial approached, the trial at the bar of public opinion went on along the roads that converged at the door of the church. To defend the accused was dangerous. By the iron law of the Colony, to speak for him would lead to suffering with him. Yet on a lonely road, and to the bosom of a friend, Dame or Goodman Puritan might safely defend Roger Williams. To condemn him was safer, of course, and cowards could cry, "Let him be driven forth. For years we have been patient with him. Frequently hath our saintly Master John Cotton pleaded with him. Yet hath he persisted in preaching his violent opinions. Let him be banished! Doth he cry 'Liberty'? Give him the liberty to stay outside our Colony. This Roger Williams is a firebrand, and everywhere hath spread confusion; at Boston, at Plymouth, and now at Salem. He is a revolutionary. He shall recant or begone!"

But those who knew Roger Williams and had heard him, whispered the prayer: "May Master Williams be spared us," and confessed that the spirit of his words were to them like fresh wind to sails in the harbor. Yet unless he recanted those

4

opinions of his that had offended the magistrates of Boston, he would be banished. And Master Williams would never recant.

The gloomy church overflowed with people. At one end sat the Governor; ranged above him on wooden benches about fifty men, magistrates of the Colony. A cheerless company! Among them were men who denounced a stroll on Sunday as a sin against the Sabbath, men whose sole pleasure lay in contemplating the coffins they had ready for themselves, men who acted the rôle of aristocrats in the Kingdom of Heaven on Earth. They laid down laws for prayer and faith, laws for dress and food, laws for speech and work. Woe to the transgressor!

Confronting them stood Roger Williams, with soft handsome eyes and firm jaw. There were few in the room as young as he, and none as fiery. It was strange that one like him should appear in the wilderness of the frontier, and even stranger to find him a prisoner at the bar of justice. For Roger Williams was of the upper crust of English society. From boyhood he had been the friend and protégé of Sir Edward Coke, the most illustrious lawyer in the realm. As a graduate of Cambridge he had become chaplain to the nobility and the intimate of the peers of England. He had the talent and all the props of friends and position to hoist him to a footing of power. Why had he turned his back

5

on such comfort, and his face to the wilderness?

"Why?" he asked himself bitterly. Before him sat his judges who represented the same harsh spirit of persecution for which he had left England. As a lad he had been raised in the shadow of Newgate Prison and the Tower of London, where rotted men whose only crime had been to differ in faith with the Archbishop, or with the King of England. And now, in a wilderness where every falling leaf sighed of equality and every hilltop held out a vision of liberty, he was on trial for teaching these lessons of nature. . . .

The Governor arose solemnly, and a hush fell. The audience already knew the charge. Mr. Williams stood accused of the crime of preaching that the Government had no rights over the religious opinions of its subjects. The prisoner, for instance, denied that a magistrate might persecute a citizen for breaking the Sabbath. He asserted seditiously that every man or woman was free to worship God as he saw Him revealed. It was well known, moreover, that Mr. Williams had criticized the Government's treatment of the Indians. The white people had no right to the American land, he had repeatedly cried out, unless they bought it from the owners. And the owners of the soil on which they lived, and had from time unknown lived, were the Indians. Unless they paid the Indians for the land, the whites were thieves.

With these and similar outrageous opinions Mr. Williams was causing dissatisfaction with the Government.

Did he admit the charges?

Roger Williams was accused of believing in freedom; freedom of religious belief, freedom of speech, freedom of the Indians to live on their own land. This was new and radical doctrine. If the prisoner admitted the charges, how could he defend them?

The case of Massachusetts *vs.* Roger Williams was hopelessly against the defendant. The fifty men opposite him were both the Church and the Government. They were the prosecution, the jury, and the judge — all in one.

Yet Roger Williams was prompt in defense of his rights. He had no lawyer, but he needed none; not he, who had once sat in the Star Chamber of Law in England and taken shorthand notes of the speeches of Sir Edward Coke. In those days the famous lawyer was not aware of the scribbling boy under the dim ceiling of gilt stars. Later, when Roger, the merchant tailor's son, had showed him the hooks and dashes of his speeches, Sir Edward was so enchanted that he took the boy home with him and turned him loose in his library. Like an adventurous calf, Roger had browsed in the strange pastures, peeping into the dusty huge folios, sampling the blurred print. "Treatise on Tenures"

7

by Littleton, "Notes on Bracton"; odd old words printed on sheepskin. But they all seemed to deal with the rights of people. Sir Edward, too, spoke constantly of rights, the rights of Parliament against the King. . . .

The Governor demanded whether he was ready to answer; if not, the Court would be kind enough to give him a month's time for reflection. He could have a month for preparing his difficult defense.

"I am ready," answered the prisoner.

He preferred to fight his case then and there; whereupon the Court chose as its spokesman Thomas Hooker, and the trial began.

The wish for religious liberty, believed Thomas Hooker, was a sin. It meant liberty to blaspheme, to tell lies in the name of the Lord. Why had they left their comfortable homes in England, suffered death on sea and starvation in a waste land? Was it not that they as a body might worship the Lord in their own way? What! Was their agony to be made vain by a clamor for liberty?

No, Roger Williams replied. But every man had a right to his own soul. His way of worship concerned no one but himself and God. You who persecute men's bodies — remember Philip Ratcliff with his bloody back and slit ears — never help his soul.

The frowns on the faces of his judges deepened.

These were the words of a heretic. Never in the history of the world had such thoughts been uttered, save by a madman.

The Scriptures, declared Thomas Hooker, approved only two forms of government, monarchy and autocracy. Democracy was unfit for a nation. It was the meanest and worst of the forms of government. The very thought of democracy was foolish, for if the people became the rulers, whom would they rule?

Surely this must convince even a madman. But what was the prisoner at the bar saying? Government, insisted Roger Williams, was an agreement among a group of people; magistrates, merely servants chosen by these people to see that the agreement was carried out. . . .

The day wore on and the sun went down, while in the frame meetinghouse the future of America was being tried. Would Roger Williams, standing alone in the crowded house, and worn with the effort to explain to hostile minds his new plans for a better world — would he at last collapse under the strain, and sob out what his judges waited to hear, "I have sinned; I recant, and may God forgive me"? No, but he might have saved his breath. No one understood him. It was as though Thomas Hooker spoke in Hebrew and he in American slang. Thomas Hooker looked back for guidance to ancient Israel; Roger Williams foretold the United States of America. One preached the duties of people, the other pleaded their rights.

It was useless to debate further. The prisoner had pleaded guilty. He was a brilliant leader of men and the Colony could ill afford to lose him. Under the circumstances, however, there was but one thing to do.

The Governor arose to pronounce sentence. "Mr. Williams," he read, "shall depart out of this jurisdiction within six weeks."

The trial was over. Roger Williams was a banished man, an outcast. For the second time he must put out the fires in his hearth and turn his face to the forest.

II

In a driving snow the exile plunged into the forest, twisting his tracks toward Narragansett Bay. It might have been simpler to go by water, but the fugitive dared not be seen. The secret warning had reached him at Salem that officers from Boston were on the march to arrest him. He had broken the injunction of the Court not to preach his offensive faith during the time of grace they had allowed him to prepare for his exile. Now they were about to deport him back to England,

10

back to mere comfort and little hope of working out his plans for a new society of man. The course through the forest suited him better.

He was bound for Sowams, the village of Massasoit, and within four days was enjoying the kindness of "savages." The food he shared with them was poor, the wigwams smoke-holes, but he was with friends. True, he was a white man, and the whites had given the Indians no reason for trust. Quite the contrary. The wise sachems like Canonicus and Massasoit feared that the invaders would in time extirpate the natives. But there was one white man whom they did trust. Him they knew to be sympathetic. He had studied their speech and was as much at home within the tepee as one of their braves. They thought with satisfaction of his cry in the white councils: "Thieves! Why rob ye the Indian!" In any dealing with the powerful whites they could count Roger Williams as a friend. To them he was another sachem.

Massasoit greeted him with a troubled countenance. Roger Williams had arrived at a tense time. The drums of war were being tightened, the scalping knife sharpened. Over at Narragansett Canonicus was sounding the war cry. Massasoit and Canonicus had fallen out.

Roger Williams was distressed. He must prevent the war. He pleaded with Massasoit. "What are

11

all the contentions and wars of this world about generally," said Roger Williams, "but for greater dishes and bowls of porridge?"

His clothes scarcely dry, he set out for the camp of Canonicus.

At last, the common love both sachems bore him, and his persuasive good sense, brought out the pipe of peace. Roger Williams had begun his rôle of peacemaker. It will never be known how many lives, white and Indian, he saved throughout his livelong career as an agent of peace. One only knows that the devotion of the sachems to him put into his hands the power of revenge over those who had driven him out of his home, perhaps to die in the forest. But Roger Williams never knew the word "revenge." Looking about him in the country of the Narragansetts, thoughts of another kind came to him: —

"The Most High and Only Wise has provided this country and this corner as a shelter for the poor and persecuted."

The grateful Canonicus wished to repay the services of the peacemaker. The only wealth of the monarch was land — "raw land" — which was exactly what Roger Williams lacked for starting his shelter for the poor and persecuted, and he set forth to explore the empire of the generous chief. One day in his wanderings he found himself at

the mouth of the Moshassuck River, which flowed
into the great Salt River, a part of Narragansett
Bay. Heading his canoe up the Moshassuck, he
came upon a spring of sweet water. There he
landed. As he gazed about, Providence seemed at
last to smile upon him. The land rose up from the
bank and the explorer followed the rise until he
reached the summit of the hill. On the other side,
the slope fell away to the ample surface of the
great Salt River — good drainage for homes and
a harbor for commerce. Round about stood venerable woods of oak and cedar — excellent lumber
for building. Toward the south lay the fertile
Pawtucket Valley. Below, the rivers were stocked
with trout, pike, pickerel; the woods with pigeon,
turkey, deer. Providence had indeed smiled upon
him.

"Providence," he devoutly named his settlement.

He had not long to wait for companions to begin
his great social adventure. A dozen families followed him almost at once from Salem. Faith in
Roger Williams brought them. They trusted his
words — and yet there were men who without
power spoke fair words, but with power were
tyrants.

The moment came when any doubts of him
were stilled forever. He who, like the ancient
Moses, had led out his people from a place of oppression, now proposed to share his leadership

with every settler. The adventure began with a document.

We . . .

The tailor, William Arnold, is equal to the divine, Roger Williams.

do with free and joint consent promise each unto other . . .

Society, Roger Williams proclaims, is an agreement among equals.

we will . . .

Each man wishes it, freely.

subject ourselves . . . to such orders . . .

Follows the greatest step of all: —

as shall be made by the greater number . . .

The majority shall govern, democracy rule. But wait!

. . . only in civil things . . .

There was never a more startling ideal advanced for humanity, never a more lavish gift of freedom. It was every man's right, believed Roger Williams, to think and say what he might please. Only for "civil things," therefore, and never for conscience, would laws be made in his democracy.

"All laws to force Jews or Turks, Papist or

14

Pagan," said Roger Williams — "I say all such laws — are chains."

For the first time ever, government was conceived to rest on the consent of the governed. It meant, Roger Williams realized, that the majority of people might some day withdraw their consent, and rebel. But he was not afraid. It meant that when he and his friends grew old, then new times and a new generation would arise, perhaps turn against him and his laws. Still he was not afraid.

"I cannot but expect changes," he said. He would take his chances in a democracy.

The bleak men of Massachusetts scowled. The outcasts of Providence, they vowed, were marked for doom at the angry hand of God. But Mr. Greene, a citizen of Providence revisiting Salem and meeting on the road an old friend of his, spoke with such delight of life in Providence that his voice carried to the ears of the passing John Endicott. Endicott, one of those who had tried and condemned Roger Williams, distinctly heard Greene say that he would never, never return to Salem because it did not permit religious freedom. Greene had forgotten that Salem permitted no freedom of speech either; Endicott ordered him arrested. The heretic Greene was treated to the customary Salem cure. He was jailed, he was fined, he was banished.

Salem or Providence, which would win out in

the passage of time? In 1636, with the founding of Providence by Roger Williams, two opposing ideals struggled side by side in the wilderness of New England. Which could survive the test of the future? Which would become America?

III

Trouble started right away. It seems that democracy is not an easy profession to practise. Joshua Verin, for instance, came down from Salem, bringing his wife to Providence where all men were free in faith and speech. All men, yes, agreed Joshua Verin. But when Mrs. Verin chose to worship her God in a way that differed from his, the husband was wrathful. What! was he not master in his own house?

The first quarrel over woman's rights resounded through New England. The men of Massachusetts gloated. "There," they pointed out, "is an instance of the absurdity of Roger Williams' doctrine of liberty and equality: now even women claim to be as equal and free as men!"

But Roger Williams declared that freedom was not a masculine right, it was a human right, that if Verin wished to stay in Providence he must accord to his wife the same liberty that he himself had sought.

16

Step by step did Roger Williams teach the lessons of democracy. It was not easy; much easier is autocracy, where everybody knows "his place" and his burden. But "the jewel of liberty," as its American founder said, was worth the price of suffering. His teaching spread. Throughout New England, especially, he gave comfort and courage to the aggrieved. When Anne Hutchinson of Boston was tried, as Roger Williams had been two years before, and found guilty of her beliefs and banished, she and her group of thirty promptly followed the track of Roger Williams. It was good to inhale the free air of Providence. There she found her neighbor, William Coddington, also seeking advice from Roger Williams. That was ironic, because Coddington had been one of the fifty men who had banished Roger Williams. Now he and his group were deserting Boston. Where would Mr. Williams advise them to settle? Would Mr. Williams help him secure land from the Indian sachems?

Of course he would. The island of Aquidneck, suggested Roger Williams, calling it "Rhode Island," was suitable. He would see Canonicus and the other sachems concerned, about the sale of Rhode Island.

The result was that Anne Hutchinson and William Coddington and all their followers founded Portsmouth and Newport. Presently another lib-

17

erty-lover founded Warwick. Thus the spirit of Roger Williams spread. Borne from Providence, the seeds of his doctrines took root and bloomed in the adjacent hills and valleys. Feeling their common bond, the towns of Providence, Portsmouth, Newport, and Warwick united into one democratic state — a prophecy of the United States of America. Even more prophetic was the Constitution of the "Providence Plantations," — later to become the state of Rhode Island, — with its guarantees of democracy and of human rights. "The shelter for the poor and persecuted" began to grow spacious and inviting.

There came in Massachusetts a moment of great excitement. In 1649 a Dutchman, Solomon Franco, was among the immigrants to New England. Once many of the Puritans, as exiles from England, had taken refuge in Holland, so that to welcome Franco would have been only an act of common gratitude. But the Puritans discovered about the immigrant something that made them jump to bolt their doors: Franco was a Jew. That made him as unwelcome as a citizen of Providence, and the Puritans drove him out.

From England, too, the Jews had been excluded for almost four centuries. What said the voice of America to them?

"Go back where you came from," said the Boston men to Franco, and they put him on a boat bound for Holland.

Down the coast at New Amsterdam, the Dutch Americans forbade synagogues, drove out a good many Jews, and barred further Jewish immigration.

But this was not the new tone of America, not the voice of the clear and fresh earth. It was rather an echo of the old world of swarming highways and stone walls and small hope.

The real America spoke through the voice of Roger Williams.

"What horrible oppressions and horrible slaughter have the Jews suffered from the Kings and the people of this nation," he exclaimed once on a visit to London. "Let the Jews," he demanded, "be permitted to live freely and peaceably in England."

Responding to his invitation, Jewish families began to arrive in Rhode Island in 1658. From Holland, from New Amsterdam, and from Curaçao in the West Indies they came. The first Star of David appeared in the new world on the synagogue of the congregation of "Jeshuat Israel," at Newport. The poor and persecuted had found shelter.

Shrieks of pain again rang through the forest. In Boston, men and also women were being thrown into prison; were being dragged through the snow, stripped and flogged; were being hanged. It all began one summer day when the *Swallow* docked at Boston. Two English women passengers who got

19

off were seized and thrust into jail. Shortly after, upon another ship's arriving from London, four men and four women passengers were arrested and treated likewise. What, then, was their crime? They were Quakers. For that they were scourged and driven out of Massachusetts Bay, Plymouth, Connecticut; out of every New England Colony but one.

To the Quakers as to the Jews, Rhode Island held open its door and in Rhode Island the Quakers found refuge. The men of Massachusetts demanded angrily that Rhode Island expel the Quakers. But the disciples of Roger Williams replied that they could not.

"We have no law on our books," they said proudly, "to punish anybody for his faith."

In Roger Williams' state there was no persecution.

IV

The Elders of Massachusetts Bay felt that the democracy of Rhode Island was an unholy thing. They viewed the weal of Roger Williams' people with gloom. Over in England, too, the leaders ranted against him.

"He teaches disobedience to princes," said an outraged member of Parliament in the midst of

20

their struggle against the tyrant, Charles. "Roger Williams would break up our society. Parliament must take measures to defend England." It did. It ordered the public hangman to burn the fiery book in which Roger Williams declared for liberty and equality and more such revolutionary doctrine. To the fire the executioner cast the paper of "The Bloudy Tenent," and its words have been flaming ever since.

What does he say there?

The story he tells is old to-day, but refreshing to hear again. It is like a favorite song, a gay marching tune, ever stirring to the blood. It tells first how nature meant you and me to be free. "The people of this earth are not born slaves and villains," Roger Williams puts it. "We are peers." It goes on to tell how you and I and others come together and agree to form a society. "Let each of us," we say, "for our common good give up certain of our impulses. I shall not, for instance, harm you or yours, and you shall be as generous." We agree. So we draw up our Government. These rights we keep; those we consent to part with.

"I desire not that liberty for myself," Roger Williams taught, "which I would not gladly and impartially weigh out to all."

But, he warns, let there be no misunderstanding. The Government is our creature. We made it. We may change it when we see fit. Its officers have we chosen. Let them ever remember they are our servants; their duty to preserve our greatest good, peace; and in all things to have in mind the welfare of all of us. Let them never fall into the error of posing as our masters.

Roger Williams, the frontiersman, spoke not alone to his fellow pioneers in the New World. He prophesied to a world old in persecution and strife, a world which listened as to a madman. Therefore there is a monumental statue in Geneva, Switzerland, home of the League of Nations. It is the figure of the divine "madman," Roger Williams, whose faith became the faith of the civilized world.

To Americans especially, when he died in 1683, this first statesman of the New World bequeathed his ideals. Not even to-day, however, has America realized its full share of his legacy. Almost a century had to roll away before his American ideal of freedom of speech and faith could become real, before Thomas Jefferson could write "When in the course of human events . . . ," and the proud words of a democracy be written: "We, the people of the United States . . ." Almost two centuries had to pass before his plea for the abolition of human slavery could win. And his ideal of peace has yet to be unrolled in the book of the ages where Roger Williams saw it spread.

22

2

The Arch-Rebel

THOMAS JEFFERSON

A century or more after Roger Williams was born, the revolutionary spirit raised up its most valiant champion. Like Roger Williams, THOMAS JEFFERSON was well-to-do and risked everything for his faith in the equality of men. Among his kind in society, he and his doctrine were looked upon with hostility. Democracy, it was felt, was a rash experiment; "the people" were not to be trusted, must be kept in leash. To most people in America, as to the king in England, this champion threw down the challenge.

THE ARCH–REBEL

ON the second floor of Graff's, the bricklayer's house on High Street, in Philadelphia, a man sat writing. His red hair fell loosely over his forehead, and, in the manner of the day, was pigtailed against the nape of his neck. His face was long and broad, and his long thin frame drooped loosely over the sheets on the desk. His pen hung meditatively.

The window was open to relieve the June heat. But only the tap of feet on the brick pavement outside or a tremor of leaves now and then penetrated the thought in the room. The thick end of the town lay to the east, where, replacing the lawns guarded by sunflowers, rose fashionable dwellings and taverns. Lower down, in the alleys and on the docks were the frame lodgings of the humbler folk.

The City Tavern at Second and Chestnut was busier than usual. Its custom was the best in town; in fact now, during the session of the Colonial

Congress, the best in America. Merchants in good broadcloth gave the room an air of sober sense and reliability, while dandies in peach-bloom coats and gold knee-buckles supplied the gaiety. The talk floated over the dishes of sprats and tankards of ale. There could be only one topic, the same that was being thrashed by the hucksters and mechanics in the grogshops on the wharf. The man in the room at the other end of town was polishing it in the wheels of his mind.

"All men," he wrote precisely, "are created equal and independent." He crossed out "and independent." Men in a society, he reasoned, cannot live independently of one another. They merely have equal rights.

"Rights of humanity!" the man in broadcloth at the City Tavern was saying. "This is not a matter of humanity. This is a business matter — taxes, the rights of trade."

"Inalienable rights," wrote the quiet lodger on High Street, "among which are the preservation of life, of liberty . . ." He stopped. The passage lacked force. "Among these," he revised, "are life, liberty, and the pursuit of happiness. . . ." He liked the phrase: "the pursuit of happiness"! For the first time in history it was being said officially that people have a right to be happy; that they built governments to be happier. In Europe, statesmen seemed to believe that people in the far past

26

had formed governments to suffer and to die for them. America would stand on the right to be happy for one's country.

The man who so wrote and thought was just then very unhappy. His mother had recently died, a baby child of his had died, and his wife at home in Virginia lay dangerously sick.

"But," urged the man in broadcloth at the City Tavern, "we can bring Parliament to terms without prating of Liberty and Independence. I tell you, sir, this is no time to trifle with the Empire. Suppose we are independent, what then? Can we buy drygoods cheaper in France? Can you say what the French would give for our lumber and wheat?"

The red-haired man in High Street was thinking of the British Troops overrunning America on the hunt for "rebels"; of Lexington the year before; of the American merchants who, to carry on their business, were forced to become smugglers; of the British Governor of Virginia putting muskets in the hands of the slaves and spurring them against the "rebel" planters. They had burned Norfolk; they might be razing his own Monticello! He had just written that whenever men felt that their government was destroying their chance for liberty and happiness they had a right to change it. Rebellion, he thought, was one of the inalienable rights, and the time for rebellion had come to

27

America. The alarm was struck by the invasion of the British Army and by the stubbornness of George, the man who was then sitting on the throne of England.

In the grog shops on the wharf the men drank to the toast: "Down with the tyrant George! To Independence!"

Up on the hill, the cautious merchants said, "We ought to send another petition to the King."

With suppressed fury the red-haired man in the room among the trees on High Street, hurled his charges at the King. His pen was like the accusing finger of a prosecuting attorney. With mounting violence he piled up the guilt of the King. Solemnly, in the suit of the people against the King, the accountant of Liberty added up the bill of indictment. As cold as steel the lodger on High Street laid before the bar of Eternal Right no less than twenty-five counts against the man who wore the crown of the British Empire.

"He has refused," began the bill, "his assent to laws, the most wholesome and necessary for the public good." Crime and again crime sank into the scale against him who had set his own single will against the will of his people.

"He has plundered our seas, ravaged our coasts, burnt our towns, and destroyed the lives of our people." For this a price would be put on the writer's head. But he did not withhold his contempt. "A prince whose character is thus marked by every act which may define a tyrant, is unfit to be the ruler of a free people."

A subject condemned his king. By what right?

"We, therefore, the representatives of the United States of America . . . do, in the name, and by Authority of the good people of these colonies, solemnly publish and declare, that these United Colonies are, and of right ought to be free and independent states; that they are absolved from all allegiance to the British crown . . ."

The city tavern buzzed with doubt. The air was full of blame for Parliament in this — ah — difference between the Colonies and the Mother Country — Parliament, not the King, God save him. The States did well to assemble in a Congress — one for all, all for one. And true, blood had already been shed: Bunker Hill, Lexington . . . Still, if only one could prevent the disaster of declaring the independence of the Colonies, all was not yet lost. Unfortunately, that is exactly what the Congress had resolved to do. At this very moment young Thomas Jefferson from Virginia was at work on such a declaration. An able scholar and a brilliant writer on politics was Thomas Jefferson, but not a safe man. A radical, rather, not to say an anarchist. So he seemed to anyone who had read his "Summary View of the Rights of British America." Maybe, upon hearing his violent declaration, the Congress would cool off.

Such was the hope of the Conservative and the Tory. But from the wharf and alleyways arose the clamor: "Independence!"

The man on High Street gathered up his papers. It was almost July 4, 1776.

II

Thomas Jefferson had begun his lifelong fight against oppression. His own state of Virginia, no longer a British Colony, was ready to draw up a new Constitution, and the lodger on High Street packed up. The Congress urged him to stay on, but he declined, feeling that the cause of liberty just then needed him in Virginia.

The long road back home led him into the stronghold of aristocracy. Through the shaggy woodland of Virginia or along its salt tides he seemed to see the aristocrat blocking the path of democracy. To Jefferson he was an odd figure.

He stood on his veranda, adorned in periwig and knee breeches. His acres stretched wide about him. He called them, English fashion, Broad Oaks, Gunston Hall, Stratford Hall. It was as fine an estate as any English lord would wish. It ranged over five thousand acres or more, most of them in

tobacco. The wild part supplied him with sport —
he enjoyed riding to the hounds. His woodland
was stocked with fowl and deer. From his mansion
on the hill, he overlooked a blue river stocked with
the best oysters in the world — he liked fish and
fishing. But horse racing was doubtless his favorite pastime; on his pasture land, thoroughbreds
often grazed. In the midst of all this lay a village
of cabins occupied by mammies and pickaninnies
and all sorts of workmen.

A remarkable estate, but the most remarkable
thing about it was that it could never grow smaller
than it already was. Larger perhaps, but not
smaller. A law, two laws really, carried over from
Europe and the dark ages, guaranteed this. One,
the law of the first-born, or primogeniture, decreed
that in the case of a man deceased without a will,
the whole property went to the oldest son. The
other permitted the estate to be "entailed." That
is, even if the oldest son wished to be generous
to his brothers and sisters, he could not. The
"law of entail" forbade him to grant or sell any
part of the land. This created two classes of people
in Virginia: a class of powerful landlords, and a
class of people without land. Under such law,
Jefferson knew, democracy was impossible.

The aristocrat of Virginia rejected democracy
even further. His law permitted no freedom of religion. He worshiped according to the Church of

England, the Episcopalian, and made heresy against his church a crime to be punished at the stake. Quaker immigrants he flayed or drove out. Harmless heretics he did not molest but he taxed them for the support of his church. Jews, Quakers, Baptists — all had to pay the church of Virginia. It was a crime not to baptize a child Episcopalian. One could not even be married, except by an Episcopalian minister. Heaven, for the gentleman from Virginia, was exclusively an Episcopalian domain. For him, Roger Williams had never lived. So behind the walls of his estate and his church, the Virginia gentry defied the spirit of liberty.

The former lodger on High Street, Philadelphia, took rooms in Williamsburg, and again sat down to write. As a member of the Virginia Legislature he, together with a few friends, framed laws making it possible to break up big estates, and laws to guarantee religious freedom. To some it seemed that Jefferson was uprooting society.

"At least," they pleaded regarding the law of the first-born, "let us keep the old biblical law and let the oldest son have twice as much as the rest."

"No," said Jefferson, "not unless he can eat twice as much or work twice as hard."

In one more part of the world, free faith and more equal opportunity had become facts.

The aristocrats were puzzled. "Jefferson is no fool," they agreed. "But how can he believe in

32

democracy? Look at those backwoodsmen, at those mechanics. Are they fit to govern themselves, not to say us? What do they know of government?"

"They can learn," rejoined Thomas Jefferson. As for their being poor, wealth was never synonymous with talent. History was proof that the wealthy few had failed at government. It was time to give humble folk a chance. And with education they would succeed. Without education, it was true, they would be helpless in the hands of dishonest leaders. Education was necessary. The defense of the republic lay not in arsenals, but in public schools. And as yet there were no free public schools; education was still the privilege of the rich.

"Here, therefore," Jefferson offered — "here is a bill to start popular education in Virginia."

The periwigged men in knee breeches hailed his gift with silence and hostility. The bill proclaimed education as another of the rights of the people; but Jefferson thought it a necessity. He provided for free, common school training for the poor as for the rich, for girls as for boys; he provided a scheme of free scholarships to college for the best students. He provided for a public library and public art galleries.

"But who is to pay for all this?" demanded the aristocrats.

"You who own property," Jefferson proposed calmly.

This was Thomas Jefferson's answer to the enemies of democracy. Free education was the arsenal with which the American Republic would defend itself against crowns. But the bill was not then made law. It rested a prophecy, and an image of the future; more evidence that Thomas Jefferson was a man for the people.

Against him the men of wealth lined up. One of them, in 1781 when Jefferson was Governor of Virginia, went so far as to move in the Virginia Legislature that a dictator be appointed. The lives and the fortunes of the citizens, the motion read, should be at the mercy of the dictator; he himself was to be answerable to no one; his will should be law. The pretext for the motion was the crisis of war. A man rose to second the motion. The same man had once cried, "Give me Liberty or give me Death!"

Jefferson was shocked. "Is this," he reflected sadly, "the reason for giving up our lives at Bunker Hill, and Valley Forge? What contempt do these men have for our people that they would have their necks chained under the sword of a dictator! The very thought is treason against mankind. But," he warned, "let those who think that they have the right to hand over the people's government, let them be sure that the people will bend their necks

34

at the nod of a dictator. I, for one, hope that they
will not. . . ."

The motion was just barely defeated. Still some
protested. "A democracy is too slow and corrupt,"
they said. What was the remedy?

"More democracy," said Thomas Jefferson. He
hated anything that smelled of the oppression of
the Old World. As in a dream he saw his America
of the future. He saw it filled with people and with
happiness; with happiness because it was at peace
with all the world. It was wise, was his America,
and knew that wars never repay even their money
costs, let alone their suffering. Then everyone had
his farm; no slaves writhed at the bottom, no
aristocrats danced at the top. Everywhere in the
land he foresaw pleasure in art and power in
science. This was no dream passing in the night.
It was the American ideal in Jefferson's heart, the
ideal society to be built by architects like him. The
foundation was already laid. But the work was
hard and the enemy was on the watch to destroy
his plans.

III

One winter's morning toward the end of the year
1789, a ship drove into the port of Norfolk, Virginia, and a passenger stepped ashore thanking

God that he was home in America. It was Thomas Jefferson returned from France, where for five years he had served as the envoy of the United States.

"My God!" he felt, "how little do my countrymen know what precious blessings they are in possession of."

He had seen in France that which made him adore the very soil of America. For five years he had lived in the midst of human misery. He had seen at the head of twenty million people a stupid and drunken king, a silly queen, a selfish nobility with swords at the throats of a nation of serfs. He had been where a Protestant was not allowed to think or to pray; where a friend of his — a French writer — had spent thirty-five years in prison for being disrespectful to the king's sweetheart. And everywhere, ignorance and misery . . .

"Good Lord," he prayed, "deliver us from these animals of prey called kings."

He had rejoiced in the Revolution of France. With his own eyes had he witnessed the fury of the mobs in Paris. But he had hoped that liberation could come for them without bloodshed. Statesmen of France, knowing Thomas Jefferson as the great student of human liberty, had appealed to him for advice. He had responded gladly by writing for them a plan of democracy which, had they accepted it, would have saved the King's life. His old friend Lafayette, frantic to reform his government, had brought to his house French patriots. Thomas Jefferson would guide them, as he had guided the American Revolutionists. And proudly had Jefferson held up before them his model of democracy — the United States.

But when he stepped ashore that cold morning, he found his country changed. The glorious spirit of '76 seemed forgotten. Wherever Jefferson turned he was struck with the same courtly airs, the laces and frills, that had once surrounded the royal governors. John Adams, the vice-president, wondered whether George Washington should not be called Majesty or Excellence or Most Honorable, or His Highness. And Alexander Hamilton had proposed the scheme of appointing the President and the Senators for life, and of empowering the President to appoint the State Governors for life. Republics, they agreed, were bad. God save us from democracy.

"England should be our model," said John Dickinson of Philadelphia. "We need a king." Like girls sighing over pressed flowers, some regretted England and thought America ought to petition Parliament to take her back.

In such an atmosphere, Thomas Jefferson gasped. His boyhood in buckskin among the small farmers and trappers of the Virginia uplands did not fit him for it. He still throbbed with pride in the Declara-

37

tion of Independence. And his heart, like his clothes, was still free of laces and frills, and still with the mass of small farmers and mechanics.

He had come back from France intending to retire from public life and play his fiddle and work his farm at Monticello. But the country needed him now more than ever. President Washington, he was informed, had appointed him Secretary of State. He accepted. The drowsy spirit of democracy must be waked.

"Now that the madness of the Revolution is over," said the men of wealth, "let us be sane again. Liberty, Equality — these are excellent words, but you can't eat them nor coin them. If you act on them you will find yourself ruled by those Irish immigrants. And as for liberty — the liberty they want is to take what's yours; or the liberty not to pay their debts or their taxes. Be warned by the memory of that pack of beggars, the farmers of Massachusetts marching under that rascal Shay, marching to the State House, crying that the property of America belongs to those who with their lives defended it. Beware of the unpaid soldiers. Beware of the mobs in the city; they must be held down. We need a strong central government and an army, a king to crush revolutionists."

Thomas Jefferson heard the brazen speech of the foes of democracy. He knew that unless something was done to oppose them, America must say farewell to democracy. Liberty and Equality would become ghosts. The Revolution would have to be fought over again. He must do something. He must rouse the country.

The enemy was united. They were but a small group, but together they met in the Capitol, they dined together, they planned, and they pooled their fortunes. On the other side were the people, mostly farmers, living isolated and unkown to each other; plowing their bits of land, fixing their fences, and laying themselves down exhausted. Somehow these people must be reached and bound with the sense of their common danger.

Jefferson sat down to write some letters. Here and there through the States he knew of democrats on whom he could count. Sam Adams was still alive in Massachusetts, Madison and Monroe in Virginia, others. To them Jefferson's message went forth: The masses were without rights; the monarchists in the saddle; the burden on the backs of the poor; discontent seethed in the land. The people must be organized. . . .

All at once the aristocrats in power, calling themselves Federalists, became aware of a voice. A new Journal, the *Federal Gazette*, had appeared, and in its columns they were being attacked. The Government, said the *Federal Gazette*, was in the hands of the rich. The manufacturers, for instance, were being favored by the bounty of the Congress at the expense of the farmers who made up ninety per cent. of the country.

Could the country, retorted the aristocrats, do without manufacturing, without bankers, without men of property?

What about the rights of humanity? asked the *Federal Gazette.*

In the village taverns the farmers read the *Federal Gazette,* and took thought. In the cities democratic clubs were springing up. The Sons of Tammany, they called themselves. They held meetings, they gave banquets. But who was their leader? "To Thomas Jefferson, Friend of the People," they raised their glasses.

"Who should be represented in the Government?" they shouted. "Merchants? Lawyers? No. The common people."

The Federalists began to lose elections, here a governor, there a congressman. They grew furious, furious at Thomas Jefferson and at the democracy for which he stood.

Suddenly the full force of the French Revolution struck. The heads of Louis the King and Marie his Queen rolled off. The Federalists were horrified. Forgetting their own Revolution, they denounced the attack on law and order. Forgetting their debt to the French nation, they renounced their friendship for them. For the murdered monarchs they

40

shed tears, and cried for vengeance on the French Republic. "Down with Liberty, Equality, Fraternity!"

But Jefferson, who had himself seen the people of France crushed by taxes and wars to benefit the nobility, could not sympathize with their outburst. He remembered 1776, and welcomed one more Republic on earth.

The murder of the king? "If he was a traitor," said Jefferson coldly, "he ought to be punished like any other man."

That was too much for the American aristocrats. Jefferson was a filthy democrat and not to be spoken to. The man who wrote the Declaration of Independence was avoided as unfit for polite society, his name insulted. In the drawing room all things democratic were despised. Even the statue of the dead, great Franklin was smeared with mud.

In the streets, however, the shout of joy is for the French Republic. The Tricolor flutters to the same breeze as the Stars and Stripes. In 1796 this spirit mixes well with the toast of: "Thomas Jefferson, Friend of the People!" He has been elected the Vice-President of the United States.

A new terror arose. In one of the many wars which oppressed their peoples, the governments of France and England were again at each other's throats.

What a blessing, thought Jefferson, that we of

41

America are so far away from the stupidity of the Old World.

What a pity, felt his opponents, we are not closer to Europe that we might join our English brothers in crushing France.

War on France, they shouted.

Long live France, shouted the democrats, and war on England . . .

The wind rose, the flame spread. The structure of America grew hot.

Thomas Jefferson was horrified. His sympathies lay with those who were struggling to establish another democracy, the French. But his first concern was for his fellow countrymen. Besides, he hated war. He heard the saber rattle in America, he watched Congress authorize the President to increase the Navy and buy ammunition. He heard the Federalists make loud speeches about the honor of the country — and his heart sank. He had hoped that America would never build a big navy to prowl around on the lookout for war. A standing army, he feared, would kill democracy — by looking with contempt on civilians, by wasting the wealth of the nation in peace and destroying it in war. For defense, the militia alone could do. But an expedition into Europe was not defense. For mankind and for democracy, Jefferson felt, war must be prevented. But how, when the country was divided on the question not of war or peace, but of war with France

42

or war with England? Either war or the cracking of the Union seemed inevitable.

The fever rose. The aristocrats, feeling the time ripe to smite down democracy in America, passed through Congress two infamous laws. The first provided that the President could drive out of the country any foreigner he thought dangerous, and everybody was a foreigner who had not lived in America for fourteen years. For one thing, this Alien Law meant that all the Irish exiles from England, even those who had fought for American Independence, could be deported.

But the reign of terror in America began with the other law, the Sedition Law, which made it a crime to criticize any official or any law. Now let Jefferson beware of his cowardly peace talk, let the "dirty democrats" beware!

The jails got busy. A follower of Jefferson referred to the "ridiculous pomp" of President Adams. He was thrown into jail. Carrying a petition for him, a friend of his was arrested and put in jail. Another follower of Jefferson published an appeal for the prisoners, and like them landed in jail. All the time the foes of democracy, Sedition Law in hand, were watching one man. For behind all the strength of democracy in the land, they knew, stood Jefferson — whose heart was now ready to break. He had never wanted to see this day when his country was tyrannized. With freedom of speech

43

no more, democracy could not last. Even the seals of his letters were tampered with; he no longer dared sign his name to them.

Once he had given soul to a revolution. The only hope now remained in his being able to do it again. And when he heard the protests of the people everywhere against the Alien and Sedition Laws, he dared hope. The approaching presidential election would tell the fate of democracy in America.

Jefferson knew that he was more popular than ever. But he did not think of himself. He would have liked to retire to his farm and his fiddle. But he dared not. The Declaration of Independence was to be put on trial at the polls, and the question: Could a republic survive? In Europe the answer was No; the Republic of France having been cashiered by Napoleon. America was now about to give its answer.

Election day. Again the struggle of 1776. On that day the voter marked his ballot for the republic or for monarchy. For the Democrats or for the Federalists. For Jefferson or for Adams. For Jefferson's platform, not new but forgotten, and built with broad planks of freedom — freedom of religion, freedom of speech, and no standing army; or for the platform of his opponents, creaking for a monarchy, a senate for life, and an army.

When the last vote was counted, there was jubilation in the land. With a whoop of joy the mechanic

44

dropped his tools. Too happy for business, the shopkeeper shut his shop. Hand in hand with the farmer they laughed and sang in celebration of the great day of the rebirth of democracy. Thomas Jefferson had won.

IV

Some people never stop doing great things. Life, for them, ought to be eternal. During the eight years of Thomas Jefferson's presidency, the United States had been growing into the most comfortable land in the world. He had saved it from the war which threatened it. He had, through his shrewd Louisiana Purchase, added to its empire the territory beyond the Mississippi clear across to the Pacific. The vision of his ideal America glowed before him; of quiet harvest, of eternal peace, and of the utmost liberty and comfort for plain men and women.

You would say that such a man, at seventy, had earned the right to retire to his farm and his fiddle; to refresh himself in the shady lanes of memory where lived forever the young man in the room on High Street telling the world that all men were created equal. But even in Monticello the welfare of society claimed him. This time he devoted himself to one of the great convictions of his life. No

45

democracy could thrive, he had always believed, where its people were ignorant. In America, therefore, the great problem was education.

The final glimpse of Thomas Jefferson is as the "father" of the University of Virginia. One sees him on his terrace at Monticello impressing public men with the need for a State University, exchanging views with scholars on the curricula, cantering horseback over the countryside to inspect a site, drawing the building plans himself, examining stone and lumber, choosing teachers and mingling with the students.

It was Jefferson's last monument. On July 4, 1826, the country was celebrating the fiftieth anniversary of the Declaration of Independence. At Monticello its author lay dying.

"Is it the Fourth?" he asked with his last breath.

Several hours later, John Adams, up in Braintree, Massachusetts, uttered his last words. They were: —

"Thomas Jefferson still lives."

3

Horace Mann Takes the Case

The design for democracy in America was drawn by Roger Williams and Thomas Jefferson. Now their plans must be developed, and wing by wing the structure built up. One of Jefferson's firmest beliefs was that no people could be free and ignorant at the same time; the school was the indispensable servant of democracy. The free school must be built soon, Thomas Jefferson thought, or the franchise would be worthless.

In a democracy, however, neither free schools nor anything else can arise by decree. There is only one way: the conscience of the people must be aroused. That was exactly what HORACE MANN determined to do in his fight for the free school.

HORACE MANN TAKES THE CASE

WHEN Benjamin Franklin was rich in years and in glory, he turned into a saying. There were Franklin Streets, and towns called Franklin, Franklin stoves and Franklin banks. For fashion's sake, a few hundred people dwelling halfway between Boston and Providence rebaptized their town "Franklin." Acknowledging the compliment, Poor Richard proposed that he buy this Franklin a gift, something useful.

"What would you like?" he asked the townsmen.

"We should like," they replied, "a bell for our meetinghouse."

There were more useful things than bells, thought Benjamin Franklin. Books, for instance . . . And that was how Franklin, the town, came by its library.

From early days there lived in the town a family called Mann. Like most, they were farmers and they were poor, and like Benjamin Franklin, they preferred books to bells. Young Horace Mann, a long wiry shoot of the family tree, spent his evenings braiding straw for the near-by hat factory and listening to his parents' grave talk of sermons and old kings. In this atmosphere the boy perceived that the library was a place of worship, and book-learning the holy mission of men. He learned to struggle through the covers of a book without scribbling in it or sticking pins through its pages. Learning was like magic to him, and as hopelessly unattainable. Take Latin, for instance . . . That he could ever know Latin seemed as idle a dream as — well, that he could be a Senator.

For to know Latin or to wear the senatorial frock, one must have schooling. Where was Horace to get schooling? There was indeed in the town a shack called boastfully a "school." For some eight weeks through the winter Horace sat on a long wooden bench, watched by a schoolmaster who was a teacher only because the rod made him one. But since he got only about ten dollars a month, the town was content to have him. When boarding him became a nuisance, off he went to flourish his rod in some other county, maybe to farm awhile or to attend school himself. On such terms, anyone could teach school, and everyone did. That this sort of public school ran but a few months in the year was perhaps a disguised blessing.

How was Horace's love of learning to be satisfied? Not in pitching hay, not in braiding straw or sitting silently on the schoolhouse bench. Often he flung himself under a tree, rapt by the flame and sparkle in the sky, his fingertips tingling with the impulse to fix on paper the lines and tints in his eye. But his knuckles, rapped by the rod, set up other sensations. Lovely melodies there were, stirring poems; not for Horace. In the private schools, where one paid, the hungry soul might be fed and grow. But the very poor cannot keep body and soul, too.

At last a smile of fortune. In Franklin arrived a schoolmaster who knew something. Horace Mann was twenty and on fire with ambition. Master and pupil both ready, they plunged into the deep part of the classics. In Latin they read Vergil, Cicero; in Greek Æsop's Fables and the New Testament. Within six months' time Horace found himself expert enough for the sophomore class of Brown University, in Roger Williams' old town of Providence.

The richer boys went to Harvard or Yale. Brown drew the sons of farmers, mechanics, and small merchants. Since poverty was a tradition at Brown, Horace Mann became one of the most fashionable collegians on the campus.

"It is a long, long time," he wrote home, "since my last ninepence bade good-bye to its brethren; and I suspect that the last two parted in no friendly terms for they have never since met together."

What mattered pence to one who dug the nuggets of the ages? For good cheer alone, Horace Mann became the most popular student in the University; for scholarship, the most brilliant. His room, furnished with almost nothing but ideas, became the exciting college haunt. There, in the giant shadow of Roger Williams, he and his friends had much high talk.

"What do you take to be the function of America, Mann?"

To this question he must have replied: "To save humanity from Europe."

The passion of Horace Mann was his pity for humanity. He had suffered himself; and once, when the others had left his room, wrote: —

> There danced the choir, and spirits damned
> Athwart my eyes did pass;
> Pale Famine shook me by the hand,
> Death showed his empty glass.

But he was rarely so paralyzed with grief. To weep for a sufferer was good, but to cure his ache better. He wrote an essay announcing: "The Duty of Every American to Posterity." Informed that he had taken highest honors, he prepared for the graduating exercises an oration on: "The Gradual Advancement of the Human Species in Dignity and Happiness."

As a college graduate bent for the service of humanity, what could he do? The law seemed to him as good a means as any for defending the rights of people. But the president of Brown University urged him to stay on as a teacher of Greek and Latin — that lore so far away from the youth of the town of Franklin — and Horace Mann yielded. Very reluctantly he yielded. To teach humanity Latin seemed to him a strange way of helping it. Nevertheless he became a conscientious and vigorous teacher.

When the steward of the college mentioned to one of Mann's students that a friend had a fever and ought to sweat it out, the student said: "If you want to give him a sweat, send him into our recitation room without his lesson."

But Horace Mann was bound to be a lawyer and, after two years of teaching, began his study of the law. At the outset, he vowed and kept the vow that he would never take an unjust case. The lawyer that did, he declared, was an accomplice of the criminal: "He muffles the step of the burglar on his midnight errand of plunder; he whets the knife of the assassin; he puts a lighted torch into the hands of the incendiary." The principle of "My client, right or wrong," he rejected. All of society was the lawyer's client.

In 1827, when the Legislature of Massachusetts convened, it seated a new member from Dedham. He was a young man of thirty-one, tall and spare,

53

with a massive brow and a high arching head. He seemed shy; at least he rather shrank from the usual political debates, and perhaps the practised politicians mentally put him down for a nonentity. But one day, in the midst of some routine or other, when each member of the House was carefully paying no attention to the speech of the sponsor of some uninteresting bill, — or so it seemed, — ready to dismiss it with an "aye," the House became aware of brilliant eloquence on the part of the young man from Dedham. He had sprung to his feet to attack the bill. Did the gentlemen of the House not perceive, he was pointing out, that the bill before them was contrary to the principles of religious liberty, one of the basic ideals of America? In view of such a startling challenge each lawmaker thought that before voting he ought perhaps to read the bill, with the result that it was defeated. Horace Mann had made his first speech in the Legislature, and then and there the politicians rubbed him off the list of nonentities.

From then on, whenever he stood up to speak, the House knew it was to be called upon to support a measure on behalf of some unfortunate class in society. Once he came in bristling with facts merely about insane people. They were sick, he insisted, and shamefully neglected, thrust into jail or the county poorhouse. What the insane needed was special medical care. He moved therefore that the

54

Legislature appropriate funds for a State Lunatic Hospital.

"Boyish enthusiasm," said the cynical law-makers.

When his client was humanity, however, Horace Mann could not easily be put off. Had they no pity, he thundered, so to be indifferent to suffering? No respect for science, to condemn a sick man to prison; no business sense to waste the earning power of those that might with treatment recover?

"While we delay," he added, "they suffer."

The appeal was irresistible. His bill was passed, and he himself made chairman of the commission to establish one of the first hospitals of its kind in the country — the Worcester State Lunatic Hospital.

So with all questions that bore on the liberty or welfare of people, Horace Mann was recognized as a leader. Like Jefferson he believed that the duty of government was to protect the weak. The voters learned to appreciate his devotion to their interests, and for ten years he was re-elected by increasing majorities. From the House, he went to the State Senate. In 1835 he became president of the Senate. The crest of political fortune was within his reach.

II

Humanity, weak and needy, arose to bid him turn in his course.

The message began simply with a bill before the Legislature to establish a Board of Public Education. There was nothing very impressive in such a proposal but it recalled to the president of the Senate the struggles of young Horace Mann. In the light of memory, the pitiful figure of youth — thousands of him in every state — moved him deeply. The ragged youngster worked in the field, in the factory; he prowled in the city alleys. His mind was confusion and bleak energy. He wanted something — a knowledge of Latin, some power — he knew not what. He needed education, which means drawing out his pent-up energy into use. What was society doing about it? Society was doing very little.

Here and there throughout the country intelligent men hoped education would be made free. But the general feeling ran: "Free schools! The next thing the idealist will want is free food! Education is a luxury. If you want it, pay for it; if you can't afford it, no one's to blame but yourself." So the rich might say. They sent their heirs to private schools, or hired tutors for them. They did not deny the necessity of education for any but

56

the poor. The poor did not deserve it. Now and then, to be sure, a philanthropist donated money for the education of the poor, and a charity school was built. Or the members of a church would form a school for their own young. And, of course, just as communities were taxed for a poorhouse or for a jail, some of them taxed themselves for the schooling of paupers. But what self-respecting poor person would publicly admit that he was a pauper and in need of charity? Wherever, then, there was a public school, it was despised by rich and poor alike.

Thus, as regards common education, in the democracy of the United States lingered the class distinctions of the old world. Against this evil the conscience of America was stirring.

A very young man, announcing his candidacy for the legislature of Illinois, said: "I desire to see the time when education shall become much more general . . ." But his name was Abraham Lincoln.

"Open the doors of the schoolhouses to all the children in the land." But the name of this speaker was Daniel Webster.

These new voices believed that the more schools the community built the fewer poorhouses it would need; that there could be no democracy, no United States even, if the same education were not shared by all its citizens, rich or poor, native or immigrant.

They thought, moreover, of the rights of children.

Such views were scouted as mere visions. The aristocrat, the small politician, the ignorant taxpayer, protested: —

"You must not tax a man who has no children, for the benefit of the man who has. Would you take one man's plow for his neighbor's field? See those hordes of immigrants gathering in our cities. Would you charge us with the education of their children? You say that otherwise they will grow into vagrants. Well, we have jails."

Even among the poor, the idea of a common school was attacked. "The Bible and figgers is all I want my boys to know," said some farmers. A member of the legislature of Indiana boasted that when he died he would have engraved on his tombstone: "Here lies an enemy to free schools."

In the whole world there was but one small area where the law provided for free schools, and that was in New England. But, as Horace Mann knew, they were more free than schools. In the alphabet of learning, they taught only the r's, and not all of them. They were open, at most, a few months. No child was taken unless he could already read and write. Finally, if lucky enough to be within the schoolroom, the youngster rarely found himself better off than before. The learning was as bare as the room; with few and poor books, without real instruction.

Schools, not only free but good! Was there in the world a cause more vital to humanity? Horace Mann leaped to the support of the bill establishing in his state a Board of Public Education. Since the law gave the Board no power except that of observing the schools and reporting to the Legislature, the bill passed easily; and, as president of the Senate, Horace Mann had the pleasure of signing it. He prayed it might lead to bigger steps on behalf of the American child, and he turned to further business.

He never dreamed that the Governor would name him the secretary of the new Board. At first it seemed a sort of compliment requiring the courteous response of a bow and a "No, thank you!" He was not expert enough for the post, he thought modestly, nor could he afford it. It meant giving up his law practice and his political career. It meant a sacrifice of comfort for the meager living at fifteen hundred a year. What reasonable person would expect one with Mann's power and prospects to throw them all away for the futile job of a clerk?

Yet, like a martyr, Horace Mann was gripped by a spirit of sacrifice. As a lawyer, what more would he achieve in his allotted span than another legal brief, another fee? But in the obscure office open to him, without fee or privilege, he saw his greatest case in pleading for the nation's children.

59

"What is the salary?" his friends asked him. "And isn't there more dignity and honor in being president of the Senate?"

Nobody asked him what good he might do. But the vision clung to him and overwhelmed him. Now he did not wonder whether the post of Secretary of the Board of Education was worthy of him, but whether he were worthy of it.

"Ought I to think of filling this high and responsible office?" he asked. "Can I adequately perform its duties? To have the future minds of such multitudes dependent on me . . . I tremble."

But one night he confided to his diary: "Here stands my mind ready to undergo the hardships." And two nights later, the thirtieth of June, 1837: "Henceforth, so long as I hold this office, I devote myself to the supremest welfare of mankind on earth."

"My law books are for sale. My office is to let," he told his friends, "and I have resigned from the Legislature."

He had taken the case. Posterity was his client.

III

Farmer Brown, or Doctor Perkins or the store-keeper Obadiah Bluff or Sam the hired man, — in any and every county of Massachusetts, — was reading, in his Town Hall, a circular announcing

60

a convention. Good! on education. Who was it that had anything to say on education? So, Horace Mann. An uncommon fine speaker; but too bad it wasn't on politics, or cattle, or something interesting. If the weather permitted and nothing more exciting or useful turned up, one might go. . . .

"Exactly," said Horace Mann bitterly, speaking before them at the hour of convention. "You are all eager to learn how to rear cattle, but not children. You spend money to keep a Congress debating on tariffs or roads, but withhold it from education, on which tariffs and roads depend. If you want a wagon built you do not dream of hiring a gardener for the job. But to build the most delicate of mechanisms, a child's mind, you hire anybody or nobody. Look at your schoolhouse with its leaking roof, its cold which freezes the ink. Have you not the vision to see a bright cheerful room where eager scholars are busy at microscopes, globes, maps, books, and directed by an expert teacher who knows how to spare the rod? Can you not imagine a school as spacious as a temple, training the children of the rich and poor side by side into noble citizens?"

In county after county a few people heard the message. As they straggled out of the convention each felt persuaded that there was a good deal in what Horace Mann had said. Their schools were deplorable places.

61

"Now take our schools . . ." said Farmer Brown, or Dr. Perkins, meeting his neighbor on the road. "We ought to do something. . . ."

Back in Boston after his exhausting tour of the states, Horace Mann would have liked some rest. But there was no time. He must bombard the public with another kind of weapon. That weapon became a famous little magazine called the *Common School Journal*, which went broadcast to the citizens of Massachusetts. In its columns, he pleaded with his fellow Americans, he stormed at them, he wept, he roared.

"Our children and our future," he hammered, "must have more and better public schools. The country is growing. Think of the danger of living with millions of people who are ignorant and superstitious and have the power to vote! They would be like children with revolvers in hand. How can we guard against this? Educate them . . . In other countries, at other times, there have been tyranny and constant war. The only use of people has been as cannon fodder. Why have they died? Because they were ignorant. Educate them and there will no longer be tyranny or war. . . . A patriot is known by the interest he takes in Common Schools."

Perhaps the reader's eye fell on another gem: —

"Some say that the poor should get only the education of a poor man, different from that of the rich. Has God, then, provided for the poor a coarser earth, a thinner air, a paler sky? Have not the children of the poor as keen a sense of the fragrance and melody of nature as the sons of kings?"

Twice a month he regularly flung out such challenges, and people listened and nodded and said, "Horace Mann is right."

Meanwhile, the members of the Board of Education were expecting a report from their secretary. Now reports may be built of a few dead sticks and much dry rot. But, caught in the flame of Horace Mann's sacrifice, this report blazed and burned the cheeks of every citizen who read it. In it Horace Mann told a mournful story. He told how two out of every three towns in the state provided no free schools; how the rich sent their youths to private schools, and the poor did without. That meant that five out of every six children must suffer the disease of ignorance. He told how in the few towns that did keep free schools the attitude of the town was that the free school was like the poorhouse, and the scholars paupers; a few months in the year would do for them; any leaky shack would serve, and anybody for teacher who was fool enough to work for twenty-five dollars a month.

"Take care!" warned Horace Mann. "A poor free school system leads to the death of democracy."

Like a giant charge of electricity, Horace Mann's energy sent the public leaping to its feet. At once various districts voted to pay their school committees to inspect the schools regularly. Hereafter books must be carefully selected for the schools. Those youngsters too poor to buy their books were to be given them free. More improvements followed; but what gladdened the heart of Horace Mann was the confession, in all this, of "Yes, we have neglected our children, our schools. We must make amends." That was what gave him the strength to go on with his work. Already he had drawn eyes and ears to himself, and from Missouri came to him the offer of the Presidency of a college at a magnificent salary. He refused.

"Oh, let me prosper in this!" he said. "I ask no other reward for all my labors."

A rich man, inspired by Horace Mann, held out a gift of ten thousand dollars for education if the Legislature matched the sum. The public rubbed its eyes. Things were happening to their schools. But how was the money to be spent? The answer to that question Horace Mann had ready. He closed up his little office in Boston and set forth again on a tour. Again he had to face conventions of citizens, from schoolhouse to schoolhouse, from platform to platform. This time the message was slightly different. He said: "When you are sick, you call a man who has been trained to cure diseases. When you find yourself in a legal fight, you call to your defense only one who is trained in the law. How strange that when you want to educate your boy or girl, you should hand him over to any numb-skull! You support colleges for the study of law, medicine, natural science — everything but educa-tion. At West Point, we the people spend more than a hundred thousand dollars a year instructing killers how to kill; but we spend not a cent instructing teachers how to teach. To improve our race of cattle, we of Massachusetts have just given a hundred thousand dollars. What shall we give to improve our race of children?"

The day before Independence Day, 1839, at Lexington in Massachusetts, the first Normal School opened its doors. Three students entered. The training of teachers had begun in America, the science of giving knowledge to a youth without re-sorting to a thwack on the head or the dunce's cap. The reign of Ichabod Crane began to totter. Also the name of Horace Mann began to resound in the corners of the country.

Suddenly the enemy appeared. He was not numerous, but he was powerful — a sleek type of individual in the shape of a moneybag, with his agents in the Legislature. He held up a sheet of figures and his argument ran: "This is all very well, this free school business and these new-fangled Normal Schools. But do you realize what

65

it all costs? Look at this total! And who pays? We, who don't care a straw for these schools, we pay. It isn't fair. Abolish the Board of Education! Abolish the Normal Schools!"

"If you abolish the Normal Schools," warned Horace Mann, "you abolish free schools entirely. And if you do that, you may as well take with it the right to vote. You abolish democracy!"

On the floor of the Massachusetts Legislature the battle was fought out. Those were tense days for all childhood and human rights. The danger passed when, by a vote of 245 to 182, the forces of Horace Mann won, and he could go ahead with his sacrifice. He had succeeded as a teacher of the value of popular education.

When he first began his annual speaking tour, few listened. Sometimes he would arrive to find no preparations made for his lecture. Once he had to borrow a broom from a neighboring house and sweep out the schoolhouse where he was shortly to speak. In those early days, he said, one didn't need the militia to disperse rioting mobs. It was only necessary to call him to speak on free schools. But that was all changed. Wherever he went he was now received with homage and love. Invitations to lecture came to him from other parts of America, and he never refused these invitations. At his own expense he would carry his message to distant parts, like a doctor with a serum to cure disease. His money didn't matter, when he had it. His salary was only fifteen hundred dollars a year. "I will be revenged," he said. "I will do more than fifteen hundred dollars' worth of good." He lived in one room adjoining his office because that enabled him, if he found a schoolroom without necessary equipment, to buy for it maps, globes, books. That left him at times with precious little for dinner; no dinner perhaps — and he was a thin, sickly man. But come now, here is an eager class of youths with eyes to open to the geographic marvels of the earth from pole to pole; there is a dish of beef and potatoes. Which is worth more?

One of the first investigations of Horace Mann had to do with libraries. How many people in Massachusetts had books within easy and free reach? The answer to this question was shocking and again Horace Mann went breathlessly through Massachusetts to disclose the shameful state of affairs.

"Only one out of every six people have access to books," he told his audiences. "The few existing libraries are owned by the well-to-do. There are, moreover, in those libraries no books written for children."

He implored his audiences at once to establish free libraries in their communities. The thought of people without books made him weep.

"Every child" — such was his ideal — "ought to have a good library within half an hour's walk of his home."

The Board of Education was impressed with his ideal. The Legislature heard it, and libraries began to grow.

Strenuously for fifteen hours every day did Horace Mann work, until his health gave out; and so one spring day in 1843 finds him on the deck of a ship bound for Europe. But no sooner does the ship dock in England than he unpacks his fifteen hours of daily toil. He must see for himself what the schools of Europe — from Ireland to Germany — do for their pupils. Perhaps he can bring home some valuable method of teaching. In Scotland he notes a very exciting way of conducting a recitation; in Germany a novel way of teaching deaf mutes. He takes note of all the educational wonders of Europe. To the usual tourist wonders he is cold. He never looks at a castle without pity for the hut of the peasant. He visits the famous York Cathedral in England and passes it abruptly with the remark: "The sight of one child educated is a far more glowing spectacle."

When he got back from his European vacation, the sick man needed a rest. But that was impossible. There was one thing he had not yet begun in Massachusetts, and that was a Teachers' Institute. It would be a great thing for the teaching profession — and so for youth — if from time to time all the teachers could congregate like doctors or statesmen to discuss their problems. He had but to mention his plan, and, with full confidence in his wisdom, the Board of Education and the Legislature granted him the time, the place, and the money.

The common-school teachers loved him. With what attention they must have listened as he stood before them at the Teachers' Institute, and talked with them about their work!

"How can we make the school so delightful a place that even the truants will come?" he considered. "What shall we say to a pupil who prompts another during recitation? How can we help the lad who copies his work from another?"

One device of the teacher Horace Mann abhorred, and that was corporal punishment. He had seen whipping posts in the schoolroom, had seen a child cower under the rod. Before the teachers, before all the people, he denounced the use of corporal punishment.

It breeds cowards, he declared. "Look at a man in an agony of fear; he is powerless, paralyzed. What must be the effect upon the delicate texture of a child's brain, when, with weapon in hand, a brawny, whiskered madman flies at the object of his wrath? To thwack a child over the head because he doesn't get his lesson, is about as wise as

69

it would be to rap a watch with a hammer because it does not keep good time."

Was this what moved the school children of Massachusetts to have his statue erected before the State House?

For the ideal he set up was that every child had a right to an education. Those people who protested that their property was being taxed to support the schools, those he warned that the rights of property were less than the rights of the community.

"In a republic, education has the first rights," his thought was. "We hold our wealth only in trust for posterity; not to advance some of it for the education of posterity is embezzlement."

He became the Messiah of education, believing there was nothing in the world education would not do. Are there lynchings? Education will abolish them. Is there poverty, is there crime? Then we need more education. Slavery? War? Education is the cure.

Those thoughts that filled his little office in Boston radiated to the ends of the civilized world. They echoed in the woods of Maine. They built schools throughout New York. They rebuilt the schools of New Orleans. In a remote corner of Ohio, groups of men met to read aloud a copy of one of Horace Mann's Reports. In England, his Reports were printed and circulated among the lawmakers. They were translated to German and French, and when a well-known scholar of Paris read them he said: "I wish that the biography of Horace Mann might be known not only to teachers but to pupils: I wish that it might be circulated among the professors. I should like to see it in the hands of every public man."

What more is there to tell of him? How, perhaps, in 1848, he was elected to Congress, and went, just to deliver a blow at slavery. How his heart, however, remained with the schools, and when one day in 1853 two nominations came to him, that of Governor of Massachusetts and that of President of the new Ohio college of Antioch, he chose the latter; how he practically opened the doors of Antioch and served its students for six years as he knew how to serve them, until they carried him to his grave and there wrote on marble his words: —

BE ASHAMED TO DIE UNTIL YOU HAVE WON SOME
VICTORY FOR HUMANITY

He built his own monument in those twelve years when he was the secretary of the Board of Education of Massachusetts. It was not so much that, after Horace Mann, the people of Massachusetts were spending on free schools double the sum they had before spent; or that teachers' salaries had more than doubled; or that the school term was longer; or that the buildings, textbooks, studies, and teachings were vastly improved; or that he started the Normal Schools and school libraries and teachers' institutes. He did these things, and more. But the name of Horace Mann is everlasting because he converted the nation to faith in free schools; because his ideal of constant education for all leads to progress without end.

4
The Liberator

WILLIAM LLOYD GARRISON

At the time when Thomas Jefferson was writing that all men are created equal and free, half the people in America were enslaved. Jefferson knew it, and hated it, and blamed the King for it. While the Continental Congress was nodding to the beautiful sentiments of the Declaration of Independence, they heard the King called "inhumane" because he had enslaved the Africans. The Congress, many of whose members owned slaves, stopped nodding. The passage was struck out. One revolution at a time, Mr. Jefferson . . .

"Oh, if but one man could arise to lay bare in all its nakedness that outrage upon the goodness of God, human slavery!" wished John Quincy Adams, a generation after Jefferson.

He did not know it, but that man, at that moment, was growing, in the shape of a fifteen-year-old boy in Newburyport, Massachusetts: WILLIAM LLOYD GARRISON.

THE LIBERATOR

I

His name was William Lloyd Garrison, and he worked in the printing shop of the *Newburyport Herald*, setting type. It was not his first job. As far back as he could remember he had worked. As a child, it must have seemed to him that just at the time of day when the river was full of fish and playmates, just then he had to scramble off to sell his mother's candy in the streets, the boys goading him on to do his stunts in the water. Fate was even more unkind at those moments when, his pockets growing heavier and heavier with marbles, and his opponents' lighter and lighter, he had to go to help the Deacon carry firewood to his customers. (That was when his mother left him with the good Deacon Bartlett so she could go to Lynn to work in a shoe factory.) But maybe he suffered most on those winter evenings when he was about to lead his South End lads against their enemies, the "North-enders," in the most decisive battle of snowball history, and — well, he couldn't, because it was

75

time to go again to that mansion, around by the back door, to get the bag of left-over food for himself and his mother, and to remember to thank them.

His first regular job, however, had been at a shoemaker's bench when he was no bigger than a last. But there he had hardly learned to pound out a whole shoe when his mother apprenticed him to a cabinetmaker in Haverhill. Sawdust had not the friendly smell of leather, and Lloyd had become convulsed with homesickness for Newburyport and kind Deacon Bartlett. One fine day he had run away, back to Newburyport, and, a veteran of work at the age of thirteen, had become an apprentice typesetter at the *Herald*.

Handling the thoughts of others seemed to stimulate his own. One day the editor of the *Herald* received in the mails a contribution on the subject of marriage. The writer signed himself "An Old Bachelor," whoever that might be, and in the columns of the paper the letter appeared.

"For my part," An Old Bachelor proclaimed, "I am determined to lead the 'single life' and not trouble myself about the ladies."

The identity of An Old Bachelor remained unknown. No one felt the dancing pulses of the sixteen-year-old apprentice.

Now began to arrive articles signed A.O.B. on all kinds of political questions. Whoever A.O.B. was, thought the editor, he wrote well. Could he have seen his young apprentice in his room at night, bent over books on politics and on history, he might have suspected the identity of An Old Bachelor.

A.O.B. was getting experience as a journalist, and what more predictable than that William Lloyd Garrison, at the age of twenty-three, should become a newspaper editor in Boston? His paper was called the *Philanthropist,* and that, too, was fitting; for he knew from birth the suffering of humanity. His own life was a compound of hunger and tired muscles and — his mother now dead — loneliness; and he could vibrate like a fine wire in tune with sad music. William Lloyd Garrison stood ready to dedicate himself to the abolition of drink, of war, or to any great cause, when the strange figure of Benjamin Lundy arrived in Boston.

They met in a boarding house. Lundy had come up from the South on foot, stopping along the way to preach. Once he had had a successful business, had lived with his family in Virginia, among slaves and slaveholders. He told Garrison that in his youth he was used to the sight of slaves about him, but as he grew older the horror of slavery had burned into him. He had given up his business, his happy family life, and like an ancient prophet had become a wayfarer preaching the abolition of slavery.

77

"I heard the wail of the captive," said Lundy. "I felt his pangs of distress, and the iron entered my soul."

Garrison knew vaguely that Negro slaves were part of Southern scenery, but through Lundy he learned more. The biography of the American Negro flashed across his vision. . . .

It begins with an American ship at home loading rum and pistols. Meanwhile, on the West Coast of Africa, the black chieftains dispatch their armies deep into the interior for the bronze muscles which will buy the American rum and pistols. Now in a chain the captives file through the jungle. From time to time one of them wobbles, sinks down, is cut off the chain and rolled off the path. The rest look straight ahead. Out of every five of them, four will be freed by Death. Only one will have to become an American.

Death did not claim all four in the jungle. To some of them life lasted long enough to be bought by the American slaver. These were chained and squeezed 'tween decks. On the passage out, the spirit of mutiny might seize and heave one of them to the sharks; another might leap with the hope of finding at the bottom of the sea a door to a better world. But more often it was disease, spreading among the heaped and squirming bodies, that cheated the American planter of his labor-saving machine.

The ship docking in Georgia or South Carolina, the white men then dragged out what victims were still alive, freshened up their parched skins with oil, and advertised for customers.

So to the New World of opportunity, where all men were free and equal, came Juba and Bamba and Yono — names like melodies they had to give up for the brisker Toms and Jacks. They were put to work in the rice swamps, the canebrakes, fields of tobacco and cotton. Bewildered by the hard work, the strange food and climate, and the haunting memories of home, one third of them died. And the order went out for more slaves.

"It is for the good of the country," said the planter.

"For the good of the black man," said the tender-hearted.

"So hath God ordained it," taught the preacher.

William Lloyd Garrison was shaken in every last nerve.

Now he, too, heard the wail of the captive. The great cause had come to him. The iron had entered his soul.

II

Two years later in a Baltimore court of justice a prosecuting attorney stood before judge and jury to charge that the defendant, William Lloyd Garrison, was guilty of attempts against the peace and government of the state. To prove the charge, the prosecutor read aloud an article written by the defendant in the *Genius of Universal Emancipation*, the paper of which Garrison and Lundy were editors. The article dealt with the slave trade and referred to a ship called the *Francis*.

The *Francis*, Garrison had written, was owned by Francis Todd. It had always been a mystery how Mr. Todd contrived to make profitable voyages. The writer had unraveled the mystery: the *Francis* carried slaves. Men who engage in such trade, concluded Garrison, are enemies of humankind.

The defendant did not deny being the author of this attack on the respectable citizen, Mr. Todd. Now was not this proof, to any reasonable American, that the writer was a fanatic and a menace to society? asked the prosecutor.

Garrison had seen Negroes torn from their friends and family, manacled and driven by the lash along the highways, or baled into ships, sold and shipped away as freight. He had seen a slave whipped unconscious. He had seen these things, everyone had seen them, and he would not keep quiet as long as he had bread and water to give him breath; no, not until he had waked the conscience of America to this bloodcurdling crime

against her black population. A menace to society?
To a slave-owning society, yes.

The jury retired, but filed out again almost immediately; the defendant was guilty and fined fifty dollars or a term in jail. Garrison had no money. On the seventeenth of April, 1830, William Lloyd Garrison was committed to a cell in the Baltimore jail. His crime had been that of free speech, which is a crime, he realized, against tyranny only. But one tyranny leads to others, he feared, and unless slavery were abolished, Democracy in America would gradually die. The previous Fourth of July he had stood before an audience in Boston, and said: "I am sick of our praise of liberty and the inalienable rights of man." What was the tyranny of England in 1776 compared to our tyranny against the Negro?

"I despair of the republic while slavery exists therein." So he felt, spoke, and wrote; and some people denounced him as a traitor to his country. But others stirred uneasily and began to take thought, and the name and message of William Lloyd Garrison spread.

From a near-by cell, one day, a runaway slave was dragged to confront his master.

"I'll learn you," roared the slaveowner. "I'll learn you how to run away again."

"Sir," called out Garrison, "what right have you to that poor creature?"

"My father left him to me," replied the man.

"Suppose your father had broken into a bank and stolen ten thousand dollars, and safely bequeathed that as a legacy; could you conscientiously keep the money?" asked Garrison.

"Why," sneered the slaveholder, "do you really think that the slaves are beings like ourselves?"

"Certainly," said Garrison warmly. "I do not know that there is any moral or intellectual quality in the curl of the hair, or the color of the skin. I cannot conceive why a black man may not as reasonably object to my color, as I to his."

"Well, sir, how would you like to see a black man President of the United States?"

"Cheerfully," replied Garrison, "if the candidate were qualified."

Meanwhile the news of Garrison's imprisonment had reached the North, and excited even those people indifferent to the cause of slavery. "What!" they thought. "Is free speech no longer an American right?"

Every day, from every corner of the country, the jailer brought Garrison bundles of letters of sympathy. One letter brought him more than sympathy — a hundred dollars to pay his fine; and after seven weeks of prison Garrison was again free.

As they swung open the door of his cell, the

authorities in Baltimore doubtless felt that the taste of prison to which they had treated the scholarly young man had cured him of his indiscretion. Perhaps the judge and prosecutor exchanged the thought: "A nice kind youth, but misguided. Well, seven weeks of bread and water will have shrunk his antislavery stomach. Behind the bars, his viewpoint must have changed. He sees the light of day. Hereafter he will go about his own business."

They did not know William Lloyd Garrison nor the capacity of the Newburyport boy for suffering. The iron in his soul had simply annealed, was already on the anvil. In his mind he was devising the armament with which to attack slavery. To begin with, as editor, he planned a weekly paper devoted first and last to the abolition of slavery. He would call it the *Public Liberator*. Surely slavery is possible only because the citizens of America do not realize what it means. Who will resist abolition when he hears, in the columns of the *Public Liberator*, the wail of two million captives? Why, the tears of the nation will dissolve the chains. Its wrath — no, not violence. Violence, war — that was as abominable as slavery.

There were several obstacles before him. He had no printing press. He had no types, no office. He had no room to live in, no money for his next meal. What of that? His capital was his knowledge of slavery; his plant, his passion for abolition. The wherewithal would turn up.

It did. In Boston he met a printer who was at once attracted to Garrison and his cause. Within sight of Bunker Hill, in the Merchants' Hall building at the corner of Congress and Water Streets, they rented an office. It was, to be sure, a garret with dingy walls and a dirty light filtering in. The partners borrowed types here, a printing press there, got paper on credit, bought a bottle of milk and a loaf of bread, and began their daily work of fourteen hours.

"Our country is the world, our countrymen are mankind," read the motto of the *Liberator* when it appeared on New Year's Day, 1831. As newspapers go, it was a wee sheet no larger than a book. Surmounting the title THE LIBERATOR was a cut picturing a slave auction. The auctioneer's rostrum read: "Slaves, horses, and other cattle to be sold at twelve o'clock." A Negro family, about to be separated, were weeping. A bidder in a high hat was examining one of them, as a butcher might an ox. In the distance floated the Stars and Stripes, bearing the word LIBERTY.

"Let all the enemies of the persecuted blacks tremble!" announced the editor TO THE PUBLIC, and he vowed never to abandon his fight for abolition until every slave was a free man. With that he put the *Liberator* in the mails. William Lloyd

Garrison, the "abolitionist," stepped before the public.

Before long people sought him, and the garret of the *Liberator* became the quarters of a group of young men who talked of nothing but the abolition of slavery and how it was to be accomplished.

"Let us organize a society for the purpose," proposed Garrison.

One night, in the basement of the African Baptist Church on Joy Street, the society signed its constitution.

"We hold that every person has a right to immediate freedom . . . , we hold that man cannot be the property of man, we hold that a mere difference of complexion is no reason why any man should be deprived of any of his natural rights. . . ."

As an organization, the New England Anti-Slavery Society began no bigger than the *Liberator* began as a newspaper. It had but twelve members whose purpose was to liberate two million bondsmen chained under the law of the land.

The constitution agreed upon, the first meeting of the society was adjourned. As they stepped out of the basement into a rainy night, Garrison prophesied: "We shall shake the nation."

III

The rumbling was felt immediately. The slave-holders traced it to a volcano called the *Liberator*, and they spread the alarm through their ranks. Their edifice of ease, slavery, was being attacked and they rose at once to its defense. The town fathers of Georgetown took the first step by for-bidding any free Negro to read the *Liberator*. An-other offered a reward of fifteen hundred dollars for the arrest of any white person who circulated the *Liberator*. True, the nation's Constitution guar-anteed the right of free speech; but now was no time for such delicacy, thought the slaveholders.

Alarm turned to rage. The grand jury at Raleigh, North Carolina, indicted William Lloyd Garrison for felony. Not to be outdone in defense of in-justice, the legislature of Georgia offered a reward of five thousand dollars for bringing in the arch-criminal, William Lloyd Garrison. Every kidnaper must have been inspired to become a savior when William Lloyd Garrison became an outlaw in the South. As the editor of the *Liberator* watched the slaveholders squirm, he felt encouraged.

Not only laws but individuals menaced him. "You scoundrel," one letter to him read, "Hell is gaping for you."

"Your death by poison or the dagger," threatened "Revenge."

Garrison's blood did not curdle, but his ribs tickled. " 'Revenge' was certainly a desperate character," he said. "He has cost me six cents for postage."

The Anti-Slavery Society waxed powerful. It spread to other cities and far places until there was no town in the union without the rousing voice of Garrison: "Abolish slavery!" At last, on December 4, 1833, Garrison called all the antislavery societies to convene in Philadelphia, to form "The National Anti-Slavery Society." A little over a half-century before, a similar convention had taken place on almost the same spot. That convention had chosen Thomas Jefferson to write its Declaration. This one chose William Lloyd Garrison.

Through the night of December sixth, Garrison sat in the room of a Negro friend of his, — the shutters drawn, the lamp throwing shadows over his pen, — summoning the haunting spirit of Thomas Jefferson to say again to his forgetful countrymen that all men are created equal.

As daylight filtered through the shutters, the Declaration was finished.

"We will do all that in us lies . . . or perish untimely as martyrs. . . ."

The shadows had vanished. Thomas Jefferson's

last sentence, too, had finished: "We mutually pledge to each other, our lives, our fortunes, and our sacred honor."

The American Anti-Slavery Society was formed, the creature of William Lloyd Garrison, its limbs stretching nation-wide and hacking away at those chains. The agents of the Society turned up everywhere. They entreated, they rebuked, they warned America. They touched the springs of pity and remorse, they hammered away with hard common sense. No one could remain indifferent. With every man it was Yes or No to slavery.

But the slave power was also growing, and stalking its enemy, William Lloyd Garrison. Learning strategy from the Anti-Slavery Society, the slaveholders and merchants who profited by the products of slavery also appealed to their fellow citizens. Garrison, they cried, was stirring up hatred and strife, was meddling in the affairs of the South which were no concern of any but Southerners. Garrison was un-American.

BOSTONIANS AWAKE!!

Americans! . . . He is now in your power. . . . Do not let him escape you, but go this evening, armed with plenty of tar and feathers, and administer him justice at his abode at No. 9, Merchants' Hall, Congress Street.

So read the man in the street, one morning, on a handbill passed to him. Who printed it? It was not signed. That night, outside the office of the *Liberator,* gathered a mob of rowdies who snarled and threatened, but did no harm.

Garrison was undeterred: "I am ready to brave any danger even unto death," he said.

"What we intend to do for the captive, and for our country," he wrote in the *Liberator,* "must be done quickly."

He feared not that he would suffer, but that he would fail. For the slavery leaders by this time were aiming to make abolitionism a legal crime. Failing that, they scorned the law. They organized what they called Vigilance Committees and Lynch Clubs, who stormed the antislavery meetings, broke into post offices and burned the United States mail — that part of it which consisted of copies of the *Liberator.* Their newspapers inflamed the people to riotous acts; their agents offered rewards for the heads of abolition leaders. A New York friend of Garrison's had to barricade his house with shutters, bars, and bolts. Another abolitionist was murdered by a mob. The storm was approaching.

At about two o'clock in the afternoon of October 14, 1835, Garrison left his house for the office of the *Liberator,* where he was to speak at a meeting of the Boston Female Anti-Slavery

Society. As he approached the hall he noticed a crowd rapidly gathering around the door. There was nothing unusual in that, for no abolitionist meeting was without danger. What Garrison and most of the gathering crowd did not know was what had happened that morning in the office of the editor of the *Gazette*. They did not know that two merchants had called on the editor and had asked him to print and distribute a handbill that would inflame the people of Boston against the antislavery meeting. The result was an anonymous handbill calling on "Patriotic Citizens" to act.

"Friends of the Union, be vigilant!" roared the handbill.

As he entered the building Garrison knew nothing of all this.

"That's Garrison — Garrison!" rippled through the crowd. Fingers pointed.

Up in the hall, he found a number of men waiting. Garrison approached. He told them that the meeting was for ladies only; that, of course, they would withdraw. The intruders seemed struck with surprise, perhaps at the gentleness of this man who had been painted for them as a devil, but they did not withdraw. More men entered.

Garrison and the ladies consulted. For their safety he suggested he leave. For his safety, they

90

wanted him to leave. But the street was blocked by thousands of people, and he hurried from the meeting hall into the adjoining antislavery office. His friend Burleigh, who was in the office with him, locked the door. They sat and listened to the roar in the street. Through the partition Garrison heard the clear voice of the president of the Society, reading Scripture and a prayer to God to forgive their enemies. From the street he heard the cursing of the mob.

Suddenly there was a crash and the door of the office shook.

"Out with the scoundrel!" someone cried on the other side. "Garrison! we must have Garrison. Lynch him!"

"You may as well open the door," said Garrison to Burleigh. "Let them come in and do their worst."

Burleigh refused. But he did remark that he would now abandon their principle of nonresistance. When his rights were trod on, and the lives of his friends imperiled at the hands of ruffians, he would defend them at any cost.

Garrison put out his hand. "No," he said. "Do you wish to become like one of those bloodthirsty men who are seeking my life? Shall we give them blow for blow, and array sword against sword? God forbid! I will perish sooner than raise my hand against any man, even in self-defense. If

91

my life be taken, the cause of emancipation will not suffer."

From the next room they could hear a voice pleading with the ladies. It was the Mayor.

"Go home, ladies, go home. Do you wish to see a scene of bloodshed? If you do not, go home."

"We may as well die here as anywhere."

"You cannot die here. If you will go now, I will protect you, but I cannot unless you do."

Someone made a motion to adjourn. The motion carried, and to the jeers of the mob the women left the building.

"Garrison! Lynch him!" The roars redoubled. "There he goes. After him!"

A fugitive figure had been spotted in Wilson Lane; it had slipped into a shop. At once the leaders in the chase bounded into the shop, and shortly emerged, Garrison held fast between them; a rope around his body. The mob yelled triumphantly.

"They've got him!"

"They are going to hang him!"

"Don't let's kill him outright."

Garrison was calm and erect. He had taken off his glasses.

"Don't hurt him," someone called. "He is an American."

They stood behind the City Hall near the

92

ground fertilized with the blood of the first martyrs of the Revolution.

A sympathetic echo ran through the mob. "He shan't be hurt."

"No," thought Garrison, "I shan't be hurt. I shall only be tarred and feathered in the Common."

The cry arose: "To the Frog Pond with him."

The mass moved on. Just then the Mayor and a force of constables pushed their way through. Garrison smiled.

"Take him into my office," ordered the Mayor. Shielding the prisoner, he backed his way toward the steps of the Hall.

A cry of rage swept through the mob. The Mayor was thrust aside, the door to the Hall blocked. The group of constables and prisoner, however, were too close to safety, and with a rush they broke inside. Before the mob could fill the Hall, Garrison found himself locked in the Mayor's office.

The din in the corridors increased. It was plain that the badge of the law was powerless to check the mob. "I have it," exclaimed the Mayor. His plan was to arrest Garrison for disturbing the peace and put him behind bars. A warrant was drawn up.

"In the name of the Commonwealth of Massachusetts . . . apprehend the within-named William Lloyd Garrison . . . and have his body before me. . . ."

But how to get "the body" out of the building? Again the mayor worried out a ruse. He ordered two carriages, one brought with clatter and show to the South door, the other secretly to the North door. A double line of guards drew up along the South door, and to it the mob rushed.

But a mobster spied Garrison and a constable leaving by the other door, and the human wave broke over it. Garrison was shoved quickly into the carriage, the driver lashed his whip over the rearing horses and men, and the race to the jail began. A clever hand threw a rope around the coach. It tilted.

"Cut the traces! Cut the reins!" A knife flashed, but before it could do any damage, the horses bounded forward and the rope yanked away. The hands of the mob clung to the wheels, its bodies leaped at the horses, but were whipped aside.

Inside the coach Garrison was murmuring: "Oh, if they would only hear me five minutes, I am sure I could bring them to reason."

The coach swayed crazily, but the horses had headway. Behind was the pursuing mob, the way was clear, and Garrison at last safe in jail.

For the second time he had landed in jail. As he lay down for the night, he reflected that the spirit of the mob would be spent by morning. Who had wished his destruction, he wondered, who had inspired the thoughtless mob? Had the people — the clerk, the factory hand, the teacher, the laborer — had any of them anything to lose by the doctrine that all men are created equal, by the protest against slavery? No, of course not. The mob was gathered and inspired by respectable and influential people who had something to lose by the abolition of slavery.

And so reflecting, Garrison feared for the future of a country torn with such passion. It was called a "union." To him it seemed rather a truce of two powers: the slave power of the South and the free power of the North. Between them was a breach, no union. In general, their life varied, their interests differed, their hopes clashed. He, for instance, was an outlaw to the one, and a mere dreamer to the other. Was there a union? Only blood could cement the breach between the powers face to face across it. To Garrison, decision by bloodshed was abhorrent. To avert it, he would advocate peace and disunion.

IV

The march of events upheld him. Even his fellow citizens, who had mobbed him and been outraged by his appeal to drop the mask of a union, even they came to see that the union could not continue half slave, half free. Every new acre of habitation added to the country became a furious battleground of the question: Should slavery be permitted? The South wanted ever more land for its slave plantations. It looked toward the North, to the West — but it found itself balked. It looked to the South over the borders of its neighbor, and, leading the country into a shameful war, wrested from Mexico the territory it wanted. To please the slaveowner, the Northerner had to help track down fugitive slaves, even to help put chains on free Negroes. Slavery threatened to dominate the whole country. William Lloyd Garrison was right: the Union was a fiction.

The threat of civil war hung over the country. For Garrison war and slavery were equally tragic; he fought for the abolition of both. He would not have his country buy the abolition of slavery with the price of human slaughter, and he tried to convince his fellow countrymen that the land of freemen ought peaceably to separate from the land of slaves. A time would come, he maintained, when in their wisdom slaveholders would set free every Negro.

But on the morning of April 12, 1861, the first shot was fired from a Southern gun on Fort Sumter. The chains were rattling loose.

Bull Run . . . Antietam . . .

"I do order and declare," proclaimed President Lincoln on January 1, 1863, "that all persons held as slaves . . . are . . . free."

Vicksburg . . . Gettysburg . . . and Appomattox.

The cause for which Garrison had given his years and all but his life, was won. Someone tried to convey to Abraham Lincoln the Negro's debt to him. "I have been only an instrument," he said. "The logic and moral power of Garrison and the antislavery people of the country have done all."

With that, William Lloyd Garrison became enshrined as a national hero. He was invited by the Government to be its guest at the re-raising of the Stars and Stripes over Fort Sumter, and he accepted the invitation partly because he longed to revisit the scene of his youthful ordeal in Baltimore. His trip South resembled the march of a deliverer who, at every step, must stop to acknowledge the acclaim of his people. The "enemy of his country" had become one of its saviors.

For the sake of old times, he went down to look at the walls of the jail, but they had been torn down. The courthouse was still there, but not the old judge. The new judge welcomed his illustrious guest, and brought out of the files the indictment against Garrison. Some of the jurors who had found the young abolitionist guilty were still alive, and the judge threatened jokingly to summon them to court that Garrison might forgive them.

He came to Georgia whose legislature had once set a price on his head. The emancipated race, whose wrongs he had made his wrongs, were delirious with joy at the sight of him. In Charleston, they waited for him with offerings of speeches and flowers and tears. They took him to their church, put him in the pulpit where they could gaze at him. Their spokesman, pointing to two little girls who stood near by, said: —

"Here you see stand before you your handiwork. These children were robbed from me. You have restored them to me. And I tell you it is not this heart alone, but there are mothers, there are fathers, there are sisters, and there are brothers, the pulsation of whose hearts is unimaginable. The greeting that they would give you, Sir, it is almost impossible for me to express; but simply, Sir, we welcome and look upon you as our savior."

"Thank God," replied Garrison. "This day you are free! The American Government will stand by you to establish your freedom against whatever claims your former masters may bring. The time was when it gave you no protection. Now all is changed! Once I could not feel any gladness at the sight of the American flag, because it was stained with your blood. Now it floats purged of its gory stains; it symbolizes freedom for all, without distinction of race or color."

On the morning of his departure from Charleston, the wharf was crowded with freed men. Everyone, it seemed, had brought him a gift. A bunch of roses, a nosegay of jasmine, honeysuckle. An old woman had a bowl of nuts for him, a young one had baked little cakes. Garrison went to his stateroom with a full heart, and laid the flowers on his berth.

"Garrison," said his companion. "You began your warfare at the North in the face of rotten eggs and brickbats. Behold, you end it at Charleston on a bed of roses."

Garrison announced to his readers that with emancipation the *Liberator* had delivered its message, and its career was finished. At the age of sixty he was without means and without work. But his comfort was now a national concern, and in a little while there was put into his hands more than thirty thousand dollars in voluntary contributions for his welfare from all parts of the country. His remaining years were as calm as his early ones had been stormy.

In Boston, on May 24, 1879, all flags floated at half-mast. The people were mourning the passing of a great man. It was odd, but once they had mobbed that man.

5

Susan Brownell Anthony
vs. The United States

*Still Jefferson's promise of a government only by con-
sent of the governed was unredeemed in America. One
half of the people was still without the franchise. This
was sometimes called "the better half." But the coin of
gallantry was too base a payment for inferior position.
These people strove not for the ballot alone, but for the
mutual respect which the ballot would bring about and
an equality of women and men in all fields. So they
hoped. And their hopes became deeds through the
person of* SUSAN BROWNELL ANTHONY.

SUSAN BROWNELL ANTHONY
vs.
THE UNITED STATES

I

When William Lloyd Garrison was in the thick of his fight against slavery, he sometimes dropped in on his friends the Anthonys who had a farm near Rochester, New York. There, of a Sunday afternoon, he could always count on finding congenial spirits. When the wagon had brought in the last guest from the city, and everyone had drawn his chair up for the feast, the political question of the day was served, and fine feelings shared. That disgraceful Missouri Compromise! That savage Fugitive Slave Act!

Susan, Dan Anthony's daughter, looked forward to these Sunday gatherings and debates as her sister did to the visit of her young man. Susan was tall and serious. She cooked, she baked, she set the table for the Sunday dinner. For various reasons the men included her in their remarks — for her understanding, maybe; for her eyes like

103

beds of fire; for the passion she shared with them for Freedom and Justice. She made her living as a school teacher. But listening to Garrison and his friends, she felt dissatisfied with herself. While she sat in a schoolroom pounding the multiplication table into the unwilling heads of urchins, in the world outside humanity lay bound in chains. In the drama of American life the principal rôles were acted by people like Garrison. They had the ringing lines ("We must break our union with slaveholders"); she the obscure ones ("Johnnie, stop your talking").

But on those Sunday afternoons during the year 1850, Susan was satisfied. She partook of the council of the chiefs. She heard all their thrilling stories.

One of these stories had an odd, disturbing twist to it. It began with an antislavery convention held at London in 1840. Garrison, one of the speakers on the program, had sailed to England. So had other Americans, including several women delegates from Garrison's Anti-Slavery Society. Garrison's ship being delayed at sea, he arrived late: the convention had begun its deliberation. Garrison was about to take his seat when he learned that all his women friends had been excluded from the convention. The reason given for excluding the women was that they were women. It was an outrage, said Garrison, and he refused to take his

104

part in the convention. But the American women had reacted differently. "We are striving to gain Freedom and Equality for Negroes," they said. "We must first get them for ourselves."

Susan was shocked. She had read of a convention of women at Seneca Falls on July 14, 1848. She herself had not attended, but knew that there had been talk of "woman's rights"; that the woman's "declaration of independence" had been written.

"Those women are doing the right thing," thought Susan. "But, after all, the crime to-day is slavery. We must first free the slave. Women's rights can wait."

Not long after, she was invited to a meeting of the Sons of Temperance. A motion on the floor interesting her, she arose to speak.

"Order!" rapped the president. "The sisters are not invited to speak, but to listen and learn."

Susan left at once. She had learned enough.

Another time she sat in the hall of the New York State Legislature when a petition with twenty-eight thousand names was being discussed. One speaker picked up the petition, ran through it with his eye, and flung it to the floor. "They are only women and children," he exclaimed.

Susan left thoughtfully. Women, then, were not the equal of men. Why? As a child she had seen women working in her father's cotton mill. They earned their way. She herself had worked in the fields alongside her brother. At school she had been as good a student as her brother. When her father had lost his money, she had helped support the family with her salary from teaching. Was she not as good as a man teacher? No one denied that she was. Yet her salary was only one fourth the man's. As a citizen her brother was free to vote; not she. Even her name on a petition was treated with contempt.

Susan was indignant not for herself, but for womankind. Among the well-born, the male bowed to the female and had a gallant word on his lips. To him she was a clinging creature who sometimes burst into tears and now and then fainted for him. Among the lowly, the female was fit for only rough work or sewing. The professions were closed to her. There were no colleges, no high schools even, for her. She was considered unfit for learning. But in England they used women like horses to pull trams in the mines.

This is a man's world, thought Susan Anthony. Married women were not allowed control over their own property, their own wages, even their own children. The husband was the absolute ruler of the roost. Single women were despised as "old maids." Though the law allowed her to transact her own business, or be out of doors after dark without an escort she was viewed with contempt. In the man's world, single women were as bound as married women.

Susan writhed. Women were worse off than slaves. Slaves could escape. Slaves had their champions like William Lloyd Garrison who in time would win their freedom. Women had no refuge. No one raised the cry: Freedom and Equality for Women. No one quoted the Declaration of Independence in their behalf.

Ah, yes. She had forgotten the Seneca Falls Convention in July 1848. What was said there?

"We hold these truths to be self-evident: that all men and women are created equal. . . .

"The history of mankind is a history of repeated injuries and usurpations on the part of man toward women. . . .

"He has compelled her to submit to laws, in the formation of which she has no voice. . . .

"He has withheld from her rights which are given to the most ignorant and degraded men. . . ."

All her pulses quickened in Susan Anthony, as never before. She felt like a Colonist in '76 listening to Thomas Jefferson. In the name of womankind she heard the call to revolution, and she determined to give up everything to enlist in the cause.

II

Mr. John Doe, America's average citizen, began frequently to read in his newspaper about meetings of women.

MISS SUSAN B. ANTHONY ON THE STUMP

Among the remedies which she suggested for the evils which she alleges to exist, are complete enfranchisement of women. . . . Miss Anthony may be a very respectable lady, but such conversation is certainly not calculated to enhance public regard for her. . . .

At first John Doe laughs. Even Mrs. John Doe laughs. "What strange females there are," she says, referring to Miss Anthony and her kind. They agree with their newspapers, which one morning announces: —

BATTLE OF THE SEXES

By her nature, her sex, woman is doomed to subjection. . . . What do the leaders of women's rights conventions want? They want to vote . . . to be members of Congress . . . to be lawyers, doctors. How funny!

108

The John Does become acquainted with the name of Susan Anthony. She seems to be the arch-rebel against Mr. Doe's domestic supremacy.

One night, a cold and stormy one perhaps, there is a knock at the door. A stranger stands on the step.

"Good evening." It is a woman. "I represent the Women's Rights Movement."

One of Susan Anthony's army, trudging from house to house, beseeching signatures to her petition. The John Does, as like as not, are ready to slam the door in her face.

"But," pleads the agent of Women's Rights, "our Declaration of Independence distinctly states that governments derive their just powers from the consent of the governed. Yet our government does not ask the consent of the governed women."

Mrs. John Doe may remark that she is content to rely on her husband's judgment at the polls. He loves her; he provides for her.

"But," the agent points out, "many women are not married; many are widows who must work and rear children. Besides, not all married women are so lucky as to be provided for."

Whether they sign the petition or not, the John Does cannot help but be impressed.

Susan herself, in 1855, canvassed all the counties of the State of New York. Throughout all the small towns she hired halls, hung her posters, conducted the meetings, and circulated her petitions.

"What we ask in one petition," she explained to her audiences, "is the right for working married women to their wages, and equal control over her children. In this other petition, we ask the right to vote."

Then gathering up all her petitions she went before the Legislature in Albany. Year after year her strategy was the same: to canvass, to lecture, to bear petitions to the Legislature. In those early days she was usually met with derision or scorn. Presenting her rolls of signatures to the Legislature at Albany, she had to steel herself against certain failure.

The chairman of the New York Senate Judiciary Committee once reported on the proposal to give women their own wages and the right to protect their young children. With a sly smile he announced that the bachelors on the committee, because they were still suitors to "the gentler sex," had left the decision to the married "gentlemen." Married life had given the committee the experience to decide.

The hall rocked with laughter. Susan clutched hard at the railing.

"The ladies have the best place and the choicest tidbits at the table. They have the best seat in the cars. A lady's dress costs three times as much as that of a gentleman. . . . The committee have concluded to recommend no measure."

With another laugh the "gentlemen" proceeded to serious matters, while Susan struggled to repress her anger. But, she warned the members of the Legislature, they would have to answer her at their next meeting, at every meeting thereafter.

She prepared herself to cope with every hardship, from sneers to brickbats. She had given up her career as a teacher, her livelihood even. She had been wooed for marriage, but had said no: she was consecrated to a cause. She was deep in debt, because when she came to pay for hiring a hall, printing handbills or posters, the Woman's Rights campaign chest was frequently empty. And, like some pioneer in a new land, she suffered the physical hardships of the road in winter; pushing by stagecoach in all weathers among the hamlets of the far borders of New York State. Her life was a sacrifice to the cause of Women's Rights.

But she was changing the mind of the nation. The John Does, increasing numbers of them, did not wait for her to knock at their doors: they went to her lectures. Her fame as a speaker drew such large audiences that managers of lecture bureaus found it profitable to invite her to the platform at a good fee. In the wake of her lecture tours sprang a trail of Women's Rights Clubs. Leaders of public opinion began to proclaim the justice of

111

her cause. Here and there a man of wealth donated funds for her campaign. The smile faded from the lips of lawmakers. The time came when her appearance before a Legislature was the signal for grave debate. Susan Anthony had to be answered. And trying to answer her, many fair-minded men found to their astonishment that they were unable. Their minds became fertile with doubt. Was it not true that men were depriving women of their rights? At any rate, observed the politicians, the will of the American people was growing ever more insistent for the equality of women and men.

At last, after the years of work, a great day in the life of Susan Anthony: At the opening of the year 1860 the Legislature of New York convened as usual to find Susan Anthony and her fellow workers among them. On the morning of February eighteenth the speaker's desk was occupied by a woman. She was not Susan Anthony. Her presence, however, and the speech before her — those revealed the hand of Susan Anthony.

"Some of you who have no slaves," said the speaker, "can see the cruelty of their oppression, but who of you appreciate the humiliation to which women are subject? . . . The Negro has no name. He is Cuffy Douglas or Cuffy Brooks, just whose Cuffy he may chance to be. The woman has no name. She is Mrs. Richard Roe or Mrs. John Doe, just whose Mrs. she may chance to be. Cuffy has no right to his earnings. Mrs. Roe has no right to her earnings. Cuffy has no right to his children. Mrs. Roe has no right to her children. Cuffy has no legal existence. Mrs. Roe has no legal existence. . . .

"What have women and Negroes to do with rights?" asked the speaker ironically. "We ask no more than the poor devils in the Scripture asked, 'Let us alone.' In mercy, let us take care of ourselves, our property, our children, and our homes."

The Assembly burst into hearty applause. Seizing her opportunity, Susan Anthony sought out a prominent Senator and thrust upon him the draft of an Act which, she said, would for the time satisfy the women of New York. A month later the Act became law. For the first time in history — in one state of America, in one part of the civilized earth — a married woman was allowed to own property and have as much control over her children as her husband had. Civilization had taken another step forward.

Susan Anthony did not stop to celebrate. She looked ahead to a larger victory. What she had accomplished for the women of New York she now dared hope to accomplish for the women of the nation, that and more. She perceived how the struggle for the equality of women and men was

113

linked with the struggle for the equality of Negroes
and whites. It seemed plain to her that when the
slave was made free, the next step would be to
give him the right to vote. For that, the national
Constitution would need an amendment. When
the time came to write such an amendment into
the Constitution, when Liberty held the pen,
women as well as Negroes would be granted the
ballot. Susan Anthony felt confident of that. The
nation, in a mood of equality and justice, would
not say that a white woman was not the equal of
a Negro man. If one was fit to vote — and he was
— so was the other.

For Susan Anthony, the end of her struggle is
in sight. The emancipation of the Negro, for
which she has worked as strenuously as for
Women's Rights, has been proclaimed. The Thir-
teenth Amendment, abolishing slavery, has been
added to the Constitution. The next amendment,
making freed men citizens — and surely, making
women citizens as well — is on its way; and then
Susan Anthony will have won her long fight. Then
she can turn home, and go back to her own life.
She is not yet old. She can still enjoy the best of
life, the peace of a family and friends, toasting
her feet by the fire.

It was not to be. The Fourteenth Amendment
was announced the sixteenth of June, 1866. Had

she been that sort of female, Susan Anthony would have swooned. "We are betrayed!" cried her fellow workers. As one newspaper said: "It was a mean thing to put the word *male* into the Fourteenth Amendment."

But it was the Fifteenth Amendment, three years later, that settled the career of Susan Anthony.

"The right of citizens . . . to vote shall not be denied . . . on account of race, color, or previous condition of servitude."

The right to vote could still be denied on account of sex.

Susan Anthony was happy for the Negro race. But after twenty years of agony the struggle for woman's right to vote was more bitter than ever. Garrison, Lincoln, and other good people had freed the slaves. Who would emancipate woman?

III

On the morning of June 18, 1873, the placid village of Canandaigua in northern New York was the nation's center of attention. That morning at Canandaigua the courthouse was crowded. Within the bar sat the accused and her counsel, and the United States district attorney. The judge and jury were ready for the case on the docket:

115

The United States of America *vs.* Susan B. Anthony.

The district attorney began: —

"May it please the Court and Gentlemen of the Jury: On the fifth of November, 1872, there was held in this state a general election. The defendant, Miss Susan B. Anthony, on that day voted for a representative in the Congress of the United States. At that time she was a woman. She did not have a right to vote. There is no question but what she is guilty of violating a law of the United States."

After dilating a bit on the indictment, the district attorney called as a witness the inspector of elections. The witness testified that he saw the defendant cast a ballot. Under cross-examination by the defendant's counsel, it further developed: —

Question. Was there any objection made, or any doubt raised as to her right to vote?

Answer. There was.

Question. On what ground?

Answer. On the ground that the Constitution of the State of New York did not allow women to vote.

Question. What was the defect in her right to vote as a citizen?

Answer. She was not a male citizen.

Question. That she was a woman?

Answer. Yes, sir.

Question. Won't you state what Miss Anthony said when she offered her name for registration?

Answer. She claimed her right under the Constitution of the United States.

Question. Did she name any particular amendment?

Answer. Yes, sir. She cited the Fourteenth Amendment.

Question. Under that she claimed her right to vote?

Answer. Yes, sir.

The United States rested its case.

The counsel for the defense arose: "If the Court please, Gentlemen of the Jury . . ." Then he proceeded to speak for three hours: This was a momentous case, he began. If his client were acquitted, the women of the whole country would henceforth be entitled to vote. . . . Now when Miss Anthony's brother voted, he was praiseworthy; when she herself voted, she was a criminal. Miss Anthony's crime, then, consisted in being a woman. Have not women the same interest in government as men; are they not hurt by the same bad laws, benefited by the same good laws? Her property, like her brother's, was subject to taxation, yet in her case taxation without representation was no tyranny. Moreover, here she was, a woman before a bar of justice. Yet she could have no woman lawyer, judge, nor juror. . . . The speaker quoted from the Declaration of Independence and the Constitution of the United States, from Thomas Jefferson and Abraham Lin-

117

coln. He gave illustrations of fine women he knew who suffered from worthless husbands with the sanction of the law. He warned the Court that slavery had been abolished. But his great legal point was that the Fourteenth Amendment defined a citizen as a "person born or naturalized in the United States." Miss Anthony was therefore a citizen. One of the rights of a citizen was the right to vote at civil elections. In voting at the past election, his client was acting within her rights. . . .

The Court disagreed. He admitted that the defendant was a citizen of the United States. But, maintained His Honor, a citizen did not necessarily have the right to vote. The right to vote was granted by the laws of each state. The Fourteenth and Fifteenth Amendments were intended to enfranchise Negroes, not women. His Honor felt compelled to order the jury to bring in a verdict of "guilty."

THE COURT: The prisoner will stand up. Has the prisoner anything to say why sentence should not be pronounced?

MISS ANTHONY: Yes, your honor, I have many things to say; for in your ordered verdict of guilty, you have trampled underfoot every vital principle of our Government. . . .

THE COURT: The prisoner has been tried according to the established forms of law.

118

Miss Anthony: Yes, Your Honor, but by forms of law all made by men, in favor of men, and against women. . . .

The Court: The sentence of the Court is that you pay a fine of one hundred dollars and costs.

Miss Anthony: May it please Your Honor, I shall never pay a dollar of your unjust penalty. All I possess is a ten-thousand-dollar debt incurred by publishing my paper, the *Revolution,* four years ago, the sole object of which was to educate all women to do as I have done: rebel against your man-made, unjust laws that tax, fine, imprison, and hang women, while they deny them the right of representation in the government; and I shall work on with might and main to pay every dollar of that honest debt, but not a penny shall go to this unjust claim. And I shall continue to urge all women to practice the old revolutionary maxim: "Resistance to tyranny is obedience to God."

IV

The trial of Susan Anthony for illegal voting attracted to her so much sympathy that although she stood convicted, her cause gained ground. Even the opponents of woman's suffrage admired the pluck of its leader. The judge of the trial, poor fellow, immediately found himself unpopular. He was like a boy who had poked a stick into a hornet's nest. In fact, there was a feeling in the air that at Canandaigua the United States had been convicted of barbarism; that in the person of Susan Anthony, American Womanhood had been wronged. In the soft light of conscience the nation beheld her, alone and proud, and lost its heart to her. From all parts of the country came donations of money to Susan Anthony, with cheering messages to keep fighting. By the daring act of casting a ballot, she seemed to deserve the ballot.

The politicians were thoughtful. "It is only a question of time," they admitted. "Woman's suffrage is bound to come."

Already opportunity was turning its face to women. Colleges were opening for them. Girls were learning stenography and typewriting and entering the world of business. Wages were growing less unfair to women. In the territory of Wyoming a startling thing happened. As a joke the Legislature had passed a woman's suffrage bill. The Legislature could afford their little joke because they were sure the Governor would veto the bill. But the Governor had heard Susan Anthony speak. It had been when she was traveling in a lumber wagon across the mud of the prairies or in a sleigh through the snows of the Rockies, sleeping in cabins and eating from a lunchbasket, broadcasting her message.

"Years ago," she had said, "workingmen had not the franchise in England. Their condition in the mines and factories was as bad as that of slavery. In 1867 they won the right to vote. Since then, Parliament has enacted laws giving workingmen shorter hours, higher pay, better houses. . . . In America to-day there are millions of women working for starvation wages. Without the franchise they are unable to better their lot. Will you help to put the power of the ballot into the hands of these wage-earning women, that they may compel politicians to legislate to their favor?"

The Governor of Wyoming had been impressed with the plea. So, when the Legislature sent him the woman's suffrage bill, he did not veto it. Nor, in 1870, did the Governor of Utah. These victories encouraged Susan Anthony to continue her fight for the goal of her life, the Woman's Suffrage Amendment to the federal Constitution.

"And it's bound to come," said the politicians. "It's only a question of time."

No, not time alone; time driven by Susan Anthony, the woman whose hair had turned white in public. She had given up her youth, the comfort of home and a chair by the fire, her little wealth. Her home was built in the future, and warmed by the fire of her cause. To the upturned faces of her audience the white-haired woman on the platform had now the dignity of a prophet.

"Miss Anthony is one of the most remarkable women of the century," people said, quoting a newspaper editor.

She had become a power in the land. Intelligent people lined up on this or that side of her. But both sides joined in honor of her. As one man put it:

"I don't believe in Woman Suffrage, but I do believe in Susan B. Anthony."

In one respect she had not changed, and that was in her daily activity. Tirelessly she organized her conventions of women, canvassed for signatures to her rolls of petitions, presented them to legislatures. Candidates for public office and chiefs of political parties were sure of a visit from her. And she was received with the deference due one of the leaders of the country. "Patience!" she was assured. "It is only a question of a little while longer."

As soon as a new President was installed in the White House, he had the pleasure of a call from Susan Anthony.

"Mr. President," she would say, "before you leave the chair, recommend to Congress a Constitutional Amendment which will enfranchise women, and thus take your place in history with Lincoln, the Great Emancipator."

All the time the place alongside Lincoln was her own. But she herself was the last person in the world to suspect that. No one suspected it until the spring of 1893, during the World's Fair in Chicago. There took place at that time the first World's Congress of Women. Women from all the continents of the globe, from twenty-seven countries, held meetings for one week in the Art Palace of the Fair. To those meetings came one hundred and fifty thousand people. Of course Susan Anthony was one of them.

At the first meeting, she entered the room during the speech of one of the delegates. There was a sensation. The eyes of the audience turned from the speaker to the seventy-three-year-old woman. Arose the clamor: "Susan Anthony! Susan Anthony!" and the whole assembly burst into wild cheering. Throughout the week she could not enter a room without similar homage. On days when she was advertised to speak, a squad of police was required to manage the crowds. She might have been a queen among her subjects. When she rose to speak, the audience rose; they flung their hats and handkerchiefs in the air and rocked the building with their cheers. Not until every throat was hoarse could she begin her address.

Susan Anthony had become more than a prominent American suffragist. She was a world figure.

She was pleased. "All this shows," she remarked, "that our cause is bound to win."

Once when she was eighty years old, and again when she was eighty-four, she attended the international congresses of women held in Europe. During the first one at London, Queen Victoria was asked whether she would meet any of the delegates. Only one of them, she replied — Susan Anthony. During the second congress, at Berlin, whenever she entered a room everyone in it rose and remained standing until she was seated. Even the Empress, at a palace reception, paid her such homage. The little schoolmarm from New York was the world's most prominent woman.

And watching the growth of her crusade, what American could doubt that suffrage for women was only a question of time? The parade of Woman Suffragists became a daily sight in Washington, their banners blowing to the same breeze as the Stars and Stripes, their slogans synonymous with Democracy and Equality, their goal the "Susan B. Anthony Amendment": "The right of citizens . . . to vote shall not be denied . . . on account of sex."

In the spring of 1919, the time for the amendment ripened. On May 21, it passed both houses of Congress, and a short time later was ratified by thirty-seven states. In November 1920, exactly one hundred years after the birth of Susan Anthony, the women of America cast their first ballot. For the first time, the "other half" of Americans enjoyed the act of democracy.

"Governments derive their just powers from the consent of the governed," Thomas Jefferson had said in the Declaration of Independence to the cheers of his fellow countrymen. But not until one hundred and fifty years later could most Americans feel that his splendid words were not mockery. Susan Anthony had heaved the last huge block into the unfinished edifice of Democracy.

On February 15, 1906, the National American Woman Suffrage Association, which Susan Anthony had helped to found, celebrated her eighty-sixth birthday in Washington. Her doctors forbade her to attend the meeting. But, divining that the hour had come for her last message in the cause to which she had consecrated her whole life, she said: "The hammer may as well fall one time as another now. I am going."

One month later, on March 15, the flags in the city of Rochester drooped at half-mast. All day long in a wailing blizzard lines of silent people moved past her flag-draped coffin. The republic of immortals had admitted a woman.

The struggle for woman's rights is not ended. In the United States, women are not yet altogether the equal of men. There are still state laws which grant to husbands greater control over property and over children than they grant to wives, laws barring women from certain public offices. So it was in the days when Susan Anthony began her campaign to win equal rights for women. "Carry on," were her last public words, and the heirs to her cause have proposed one more amendment to the Constitution of the United States — that "Men and woman shall have equal rights throughout the United States. . . ."

But, powerfully armed with the ballot, guaranteed by the "Susan B. Anthony Amendment," women may be confident that complete equality for them is "only a question of time."

6

The Oracle of Democracy

CHARLES WILLIAM ELIOT

Not very long ago, many leading Americans joined in celebrating the birthday of a famous man. The event was public because the guest of honor was one of those who had added to the strength of democracy. CHARLES WILLIAM ELIOT served in another, a unique way. He could interpret the spirit of democracy so wisely that people listened to him as once they had listened to an oracle.

THE ORACLE OF DEMOCRACY

ALL that Thursday the telegraph offices of Boston clicked with messages for Charles William Eliot. For the past two months, from Singapore to London, from Paris to San Francisco, and throughout the North American Continent, groups of people had met to give words to their gratitude, to be delivered on this day, — March 20, 1924, — to this man. These people were unknown to one another, and differed in occupation, age, race, color, and creed. They were alike only in their heartfelt honoring of Charles Eliot.

From North China a writer spoke of "the greatest of teachers . . . to whose inspiration we, although far away, have looked as a thirsty man seeking water."

From Mexico a man wrote: "I have foregathered with Harvard men all over Mexico from Yucatan to the border, and always the friendly talk, at the café table under the palms, or around a campfire at timberline, has swung around to 'Prexy' Eliot. . . . Not one of us who has had

129

the privilege of personal contact with you but has had his ideals developed and strengthened. . . ."

From Canada the Prime Minister wired: "We share America's pride in one who is not less a first citizen of the world than of the republic."

The same afternoon, beginning at three-thirty, the old Sanders Theater in Cambridge staged a scene unparalleled in its history or in the history of the nation. The house was crowded. In part, the program read, "In honor of Charles William Eliot on his ninetieth birthday," and among the names of the sponsors appeared those of the President and Chief Justice of the United States, the Governor of Massachusetts, the Premier of Canada. Down the reverse side of the page ran a poem of which the casual eye might have picked up the phrases: —

> To all mankind he brings the sacred fire.
> . . . till every wrong be righted
> He holds it high . . .
> Champion of freedom . . .

The eyes of the audience were fixed on a platform banked with chairs occupied by notable men. On the right, arrayed in brilliant scarves and robes, sat the faculty of Harvard; on the left, delegates from other institutions of the country. All eyes, however, were on the center of the rear wall where, as though set within the gothic panel whose arches framed Harvard's coat of arms, sat in a high-backed chair the celebrated man, his white head erect, his spectacles flashing. He wore the academic black robe.

"Illustrious and venerable guest." The speaker, a Supreme Court justice, addressed him. "All these assembled here salute you. . . ."

He went on to characterize Charles Eliot as a happy warrior of truth, a teacher of democracy, a seer of the beautiful life. The audience hailed his sentiments with delight.

Mr. Lowell, the President of Harvard, rose. "From first to last," he said, "Mr. Eliot has been an educational warrior. Elected president at thirty-five . . . undismayed by the opposition of men of weight . . . by the frowns . . . by sharp public criticism, he pursued without flinching the end he had in view."

The speaker had recalled a striking moment. And for some of the audience, Memory, the master dramatist, blotted out the scene in Sanders Theater and threw its spotlight on another. . . .

It is the interior of the First Parish Church in Cambridge on an October afternoon in the year 1869. The audience, which fills the church to the doors, includes the Governor of the State, the dignitaries of Harvard College, James Russell Lowell, Henry W. Longfellow, Ralph Waldo Emerson.

The occasion is the inaugural of the new President of Harvard University, and there he stands on the platform, tall, straight, young, speaking with vibrant, 'cello tones.

The audience is in two minds over him. One feeling suspects his youth, his full shock of hair, his new ideas. Oh, his words sound soothing enough to the ear. But if you catch their overtones, you may shiver with uneasiness. He has just said, for example, that the University is impartial toward all branches of knowledge: science and literature and mathematics and the classics.

"We would have them all," are his words, "and at their best."

There — a threat to old Harvard, a warning that he is dissatisfied with the college course of study, a hint that he intends to try to introduce new ones.

"Not what to teach," the young president says, "but how to teach." And from primary school through college, teaching methods must be revised, he adds.

Rather sure of himself, is young Charles Eliot. His positive nature, is, indeed, the main ground for alarm; that and his new faith, the "elective" system.

"The young man of nineteen or twenty ought to know what he likes best and is most fit for." The words of this faith in youth ring through the church. "If he feels no loves, he will at least have his hates. . . . The college therefore proposes to persevere in its efforts to establish . . . the elective system."

He is at any rate frank in his revolutionary creed. He explains it by saying, "A university must be free."

Up front, Mr. Emerson is seen to nod assent. He likes immensely the fresh and promising note in the young speaker. Whom does hope not stir when he hears the spring winds beat against the frost-bound door? On such a tide, a few, like Mr. Emerson, were buoyed high with hope that the rigid New England college would open its seed-beds, would in time, yield a better, a more extensive crop of learning.

A new era may be dawning through Charles Eliot. *May* be — for words are only words, even if spoken by an impressive young man with a 'cello voice. No one has ever attacked the system of higher education in America. Few have stood out for an "elective" system, few felt the lack of freedom in the colleges. Will President Eliot attempt and carry out his plans? It is wise to wait before cheering. He has done nothing yet. . . .

Among the speakers in Sanders Theater is a youth who represents the student body of Harvard. "Their debt to you is one they can only recognize," he ends his homage to the old man. "It is one they can never pay."

A new era, then, did dawn when Charles Eliot became President of Harvard. From his red-brick house in Cambridge, as from the summit of a hill, he had surveyed life in America; and whether he turned toward his countrymen in the city or on the silent plains, one pervading feature struck him. That was the choice of opportunities for everyone's hand and taste. At labor as at the polls, American life offered a long bill of fare suited to every stomach.

"That," thought Eliot, "is democracy."

But when he turned to his own field of work, he missed the democratic feature. The schools and colleges were relics of a feudal age. They did not serve the people with the free access of other institutions, but were, so to speak, still surrounded with moat and drawbridge, cut off from democratic life. Harvard College, for instance, lowered its drawbridge only for young men who blew the classical horn: Latin and Greek were required for admission. Within the walls, the young man who had hoped that college would free him from the rigid school discipline of his boyhood found himself again locked in the classical cell.

"How dull," one college student had thought. "Eternally to construe Latin and Greek, to work out problems in Math." So had thought the youth

134

Charles Eliot when he had studied at Harvard. In addition to the classical staples, the college had permitted him a glance into a History and a Science textbook; and, as a senior, the weekly lecture of Mr. Longfellow on European Literature. He might also treat himself to a smattering of some modern language. Charles Eliot had graduated second in his class, but he had wondered how, educated in this way, he was to do any good in the world.

As President of Harvard University, he still felt the uselessness of such education. The colleges of the country were not growing, and no wonder. To a farmer's son or a mechanic's son or a boy bent for business or civil service, what did they offer? For successful life the man would need a mastery of science, modern languages, English, current social history. Yet college did little but adorn him with Latin, other ancient things, and a few tidbits; nothing more.

"Are we educating our people," demanded Charles Eliot, "for life in the seventeenth or the twentieth century?"

Higher learning was no mere luxury for the rich, thought he; it must equally train the poor; the son of the immigrant as well as the son of the old family; the Jew, the Gentile, the Buddhist. Not until the college could provide for them all, was it worthy of a place in a democracy. By its rigid curriculum which offered the student little choice — by serving only one class of students — the college was undemocratic.

With his pen and with his tongue he assailed the undemocratic college. Tirelessly he accused. He had a mission in life, and he must do it faithfully. The managers of schools and colleges the country over began to stir uneasily. On all sides the young college president was prodding them. Now he turned up in a magazine article, again on a public platform, or at a gathering of professors. And with him always came his ideal of democracy in education. There was no denying the firmness of Charles Eliot. His thought was as straight as his figure; his speech like the steel of his pen. He would be answered.

"But," was the defense, "this has been the education of our forefathers. It is the lore of the ages."

Not so, replied President Eliot. Once Greek had to fight for a place in the curriculum; once Mathematics was excluded. Besides, new branches of learning have sprouted. The colleges, for instance, are missing all beauties of the English language. They read Homer, but neglect Shakespeare and Milton. They train the student to live in ancient Rome, forgetting that he would go to Paris and Berlin. They teach no History, leaving the student ignorant of his heritage. Although this is an age of Science, not a single preparatory or high school gives adequate instruction in Science, and no college has a laboratory. . . .

He touched here the great handicap of his own student days. His favorite study had been Chemistry. How he had longed to do the experiments set forth in his textbook! The college, however, never thought it necessary to equip a laboratory. Luckily the Chemistry instructor had allowed young Charles Eliot to fool around his private laboratory. Then, on the top floor of his own home on Beacon Street opposite the Boston Common, Charles had set up a furnace. His family, to his disgust, had feared he would burn his fingers — he, a chemist! — and people had asked in polite surprise: "What are you studying Chemistry for? Do you mean to be a professor?"

Later, as a teacher of Chemistry at Harvard and at the Massachusetts Institute of Technology, he and a colleague had been the first to insist that Science must be learned — not from a textbook, but in the laboratory — that the student must himself handle the substances, stick his nose into them, peer at them; yes, burn his fingers — learn by experience. But this step in the teaching of Science required a laboratory manual, and there was none. "There is no new thing under the sun," saith the preacher. But when Eliot and Storer's "Inorganic Chemistry" appeared as a guide to students in the laboratory, it was a new thing and revolutionized science study in the United States. No longer must students blindly memorize statements in a book; they could learn the ways of Nature for themselves.

Even as a young teacher, then, Charles Eliot had begun his reform of higher education. He started written "exams," for instance. Before that time the student was examined orally before a group of "visitors" who knew neither the student nor the subject. Another time, to make "Trig" interesting, he took his class out on the college grounds, which the class surveyed, and thus made the first plan of Harvard. No one had ever before thought of doing that. Then the seeds of his great reform had rooted in his mind, the elective system.

He was cried down, of course. "You're not thinking of running a college," the diehards scoffed. "To our fine discipline you want to add courses in Science, in English, in modern languages, in History. You're thinking of a bazaar."

"Your discipline is chains," answered Charles Eliot. "To force a boy with no talent in languages to study them, is a waste for society and an outrage upon the student. Yes, to become universities our colleges must cultivate all fields of knowledge. No student, of course, can take all courses. But it will be just the beauty of college life for him that he can choose his own fields of study."

The elective system was unavoidable. "It is not only more democratic," President Eliot made clear. "It is the only way toward a university. It will mean freedom for the student and joy in learning." He recalled how happy he would have been, had an elective system allowed him to dig into Chemistry.

In books, and from platforms, Charles Eliot impressed his vision on the country. Bit by bit he built it into the country. Under the leadership of Harvard, the colleges began to add new courses. The college catalogues grew weightier; the college plans bigger. Even music and art, as Charles Eliot advocated, at last settled in the college. The rigid chains of the old course dropped away, leaving the student freer and happier to choose his work. The colleges now more useful, people flocked to them in ever increasing numbers. Supported by the people, the colleges drew fine scholars and became seats of learning matching those in Europe. . . .

When, therefore, on that March afternoon the youth in Sanders Theater says to Charles Eliot: "Their debt to you . . . is one they can never pay," he is spokesman for all America's youth from the age of ten to full manhood. He speaks for the Junior High School youth who is happy to be relieved of his — say — Latin; who can browse in the curriculum and sample all studies to find his favorites. He is speaking for the Senior High

School youth who chooses his own curriculum;
who, in doing so, is free to act on his loves and
hates and hopes. He is speaking for the student
in college who dreams over the catalogue and
checks this course, rejects that, and so arranges
the perfect diet of the mind. Charles Eliot fought
for all of them when he attacked the old system of
"one course for all," as undemocratic. He helped
them all when he insisted on a richer curriculum
and on the elective system. He liberated the youth
of the land from academic oppression.

The old man sitting straight in the high-backed
chair looks doubtful of the shower of praise on
him. Judging by its applause, the audience feels
not the slightest doubt. To the left of the old
man sit the deans of the professional schools of
Harvard and in their minds the shower of praise
is a deluge. All of them have sent Charles Eliot
messages the substance of which has been: —

"Without you, the country would not yet have
turned out so many excellent doctors, lawyers,
engineers. To you we owe the high quality of our
professional training."

It happened this way. When Charles Eliot put
Harvard College under the powerful crystal of
his mind, he found a lack of opportunity for ambi-
tious students. But when he turned to the professional schools, he found the case aggravated.

Every year, the colleges of the country unleashed on the innocent public lawyers and doctors who were a potential menace. Harvard was not to blame for a national ailment, but Charles Eliot resolved to begin the cure with Harvard.

The trouble was, first, that almost anyone could enter the school of law or that of medicine. The candidate passed in by alleging his acquaintance with the family of high school studies, and paying his fee. The professors, who got no salary, pocketed the fees and proceeded to lecture. For about eighteen months the student sat with cocked ear, and then pondered the dignities of wooden or brass shingles, of whiskers alone or the full flower of a beard.

There were, to be sure, the final examinations. On the day of examination, the medical candidate entered a large room in which sat nine professors, and the party began. Around the room fluttered the debutant, spending a ten-minute visit with each of his hosts. They, in turn, quizzed him courteously, and, when the student had left the room, voted on him, the majority deciding.

"That," thought Charles Eliot, "is carrying faith in democracy too far." Since, to pass, the student needed only five out of nine *ayes,* and since the professors feared to discourage customers, the party was almost always a social success — the candidate passing. The graduate could then order

141

his shingle and pray for whiskers. One other formality, however, still checked him: he needed a certificate to show that he had worked with a doctor for three years; not necessarily proof that he had learned anything, or been "on the job" — just a certificate.

"That," thought Charles Eliot, "is carrying trust too far."

Another doctor had joined the ranks. But the demons and imps of disease did not flinch — that is, not until Charles Eliot stepped forward.

"The whole system of medical education in this country," he announced, "needs thorough reformation."

No great campaign, it would seem, could begin with so quiet a report. No warning leaf on the campus stirred. No one heard a cannon blast: "I shall reform!" Only those who knew intimately the quiet, impersonal manner of the young president, only they could hear the step of a new era and, in the distance, the new outfit of doctors. The Faculty of the Medical School merely heard in surprise the call of a meeting one evening. In greater surprise they saw, what they had never before seen, their president, young Charles Eliot, enter and take the chair.

The campaign had opened, and no mistake. Charles Eliot fired a round: The Medical School would have to change its ways. It was slipshod;

it served the public poorly; it disgraced the name of "learned profession"; it would have to change.

The professors bridled. Change?

"How is it," one demanded, "that this Faculty has gone on for eighty years, and now within three or four months it is proposed to change all our modes? It seems very extraordinary," he added sarcastically.

Charles Eliot had anticipated this. People clung to what they had, and knowing no better, believed it the best.

"I can answer the question very easily," he replied calmly. "There is a new president."

What did he want of them, they cried in exasperation. Why did he not let things alone? Why must he call meeting after meeting and hammer away at them until, at midnight, he let them go, exhausted? Raise the entrance requirements, lengthen the course, grade it, change the teaching methods, change the form of examinations. . . . This cool, young whirlwind was calmly proposing to turn everything upside down. Even his allies resented his impatience and radicalism.

His opponents raised a weighty point: Suppose they made the reforms the president was urging. Assume, even, that medical education would be, thus, improved. But — the point flashed — *where would the students be then?* Gone; barred by the entrance requirements; discouraged by the length of training; driven out by the stiff, new rod of the teachers.

On the contrary, retorted Charles Eliot. They are driven away *now*. A serious student has to go to France or Germany for his medical education. He is unable to get Science in America.

Science! exclaimed the old-timers scornfully — for the doctor, Science is a waste of time. The hours he puts into Chemistry he could more profitably spend learning the difference — say — between hernia and hydrocele. No, good doctors are born, not made. You can't do anything about it. . . .

Unmoved by such heat, Charles Eliot pressed on, making new allies, winning over old antagonists. Step by step, the opposition yielded. The last ditch was reached. This was the question: Should a student be graduated by passing in a majority of his subjects, or in all of them? The Overseers of Harvard thought that to hold a doctor responsible in all branches of his profession was a hardship. Charles Eliot thought that a doctor who was incompetent in any branch of medicine should be barred from practice.

On the night of the crucial meeting, when the Overseers were to cast their vote for one or the other, Charles Eliot felt unsure. This seemed to be the one objective he was not to win. Nor did his hopes leap during the debate. On this point, the

Board of Overseers seemed determined. Then Old
Charles Francis Adams rose. He had a story to tell.
He knew of a young doctor, a Harvard graduate,
three of whose patients had died. The autopsy
showed that the young doctor had killed them
with overdoses of morphine. The doctor was not
to blame, however. He had been graduated even
though failing in Toxicology.

There was now no doubt of Charles Eliot's victory; the catalogue of 1871 announced: —

"The plan of study has been radically
changed. . . ."

The new doctor was on his way.

"He proceeded to turn the college over like a
flapjack," said Oliver Wendell Holmes about
Charles Eliot. But the new president was impartial:
he did the same with every other branch of the
university. The Medical School is but an instance.
All felt the fruitful, molding touch of his genius.
The country over, college presidents and trustees
watched his reforms. By gravity, his force from
Cambridge pulled up every college in the country.
Steadily Harvard advanced to the forefront of a
world-famous university. To his faculty the president added important scholars. The student body
grew despite his forcing of the standards ever
upward, until now only college graduates may
enter the schools of Law and Medicine, and of
those only a select group.

Not only the deans of the university, but everyone who needs the advice of a doctor or lawyer, is in his debt.

"From the moment when you assumed the presidency of Harvard, men have recognized in you a leader without peer."

The President of Yale University is speaking directly to the old man who sits straight and still. "You found the so-called elective system struggling feebly for existence. You made yourself its champion. . . . You saw the vision of a great university. . . . You have thus brought closer together the spirit of learning and the spirit of democracy."

The speaker finishes amid a burst of prolonged applause which dies away to permit the Governor of Massachusetts to say a few words. The Governor briefly remarks that for over half a century his fellow citizens have turned to Charles Eliot for counsel.

The next speaker is the Chief Justice of the Supreme Court. He points out that in a democracy, where live together all types and classes of people, the greatest need is a certain kind of leader. He is a rare person. He is independent and unselfish. He is fearless. He has won the confidence of the public. To him they listen with respect.

"Dr. Eliot is a leader and prophet of the people

146

in this true sense. . . . He has wielded greater power with the intelligent democracy of this country than any other unofficial citizen of his time. . . ."

Upon any question, a word from Charles Eliot would radiate like light. Were it the issues of a coming election, the best books, the rights of Labor, the public wanted to know what President Eliot thought on the question. They held him as a sort of living crystal in which shone the truth of things. He became one of the natural wonders of New England, like the Great Stone Face in Hawthorne's story, under whom the dwellers in the valley found inspiration: —

It was a happy lot for children to grow up to manhood or womanhood with the Great Stone Face before their eyes, for all the features were noble, and the expression was at once grand and sweet, as if it were the glow of a vast, warm heart, that embraced all mankind in its affections, and had room for more.

In his writings and his speeches, he taught his public how to live, held out to them all the vision of a happy life. The happy man, he showed, has his family and his friends and books. He is a lover of nature, this happy soul — delighting with all his senses in her treasures. Life is never dull to him so long as there is a wrong to make right, a truth to find out. . . .

147

Like Ernest in "The Great Stone Face," this ideal man was Charles Eliot himself, to whom, as Hawthorne says, "unsought for, undesired, had come the fame which so many seek, and made him known in the great world, beyond the limits of the valley in which he had dwelt so quietly."

He lives, this happy man, in a democracy, said Charles Eliot. To him, life means freedom. It means other things, too; the things America stands for. No war, for instance, because war crushes freedom. War says to him: "Obey without a question, even unto death; die in this ditch, without knowing why." No, our hero hates this most detestable of all occupations. He is patriotic, of course, serving his country in civil life; risking his life in many ways; as a locomotive engineer, for instance; as a policeman, a ranger — in short, as a worker for his community. He is also a fighter, but a fighter of pestilence and disease. He struggles to better the lot of the poor, of the underpaid worker. He fights, in short, those battles in which everyone may be victorious. He fights to uphold the classic American ideals of race tolerance and individual freedom. The happy man is concerned, you see, more with other people's happiness and less with his own. He will not tolerate, therefore, racial prejudice: his fellow Americans are of all races. He distrusts any but democratic government, for democracy has given human beings more well-being than has

148

any other form of government. For these things he is a loyal American. . . .

Like Ernest in "The Great Stone Face," Charles Eliot made great truths familiar by his simple utterance of them.

Three Presidents offered Charles Eliot the post of ambassador, which each time he refused. But when, in 1911, the managers of the Carnegie Endowment for International Peace asked him to journey around the world in the cause of peace, he gladly said yes. Nobody was more fit to carry the olive branch, and off he went to India and China and Japan where — even there — he was greeted with the strains of "Fair Harvard" and a cheer for "Prexy" Eliot. Statesmen were ready with more formal honors.

But Charles Eliot was a man of careful thought. Visits like his, he knew, did not prevent war.

"What are all the wars of this world about," had said a brother in democracy, Roger Williams, "but for greater dishes of porridge?" And on his return from the Orient, Charles Eliot agreed. It was in 1913 that he wrote "The Road Toward Peace," in which he said that greed and distrust among races were the roots of war. He said that dishonest newspapers fed these roots. While he spoke, those roots were shooting up in Europe. In a short while, a body of his fellow citizens would be asking him

149

to say how America could help establish peace forever in the world.

In 1909 he retired from the presidency of Harvard and became the president emeritus. From that time on, the distinguished old man devoted all his strength to the public welfare. Now it was the cause of sanitation, now the Civil Service, better city government, better conditions for workers. It was as though single-handed he would build the millennium. In 1923, the New York Civic Forum awarded him its medal of honor. He was thankful, and added the medal to the high pile of his honorary trophies.

"He is the only man in the world I envy," President Theodore Roosevelt once said.

As the Chief Justice said: "He has wielded greater power with the intelligent democracy of this country than any other unofficial citizen of his time."

In Sanders Theater the speakers have all finished. The program in the hands of the audience calls for a "Response" from Charles William Eliot. The audience leans forward.

From the high-backed chair in the center, the old man rises. The rafters begin to thunder. He steps forward — erect as the day, more than a half-century gone, when he stood before the public as the new college president. The applause is

150

deafening. This is the man who built a great university, the man whose work went into all the universities of the country. The people of the audience show their feeling toward him who has reared them sound scholars, and enriched the whole country with fine technicians, doctors, lawyers, engineers. He stands before them: patient, white-haired, his spectacles beaming. America is wonderful with its swell of prairie, its pioneers, its grand peaks, its Charles Eliot. He is their teacher, their guide, and they will not restrain their applause of him. Outside, two thousand bareheaded students wait for him in the yard, for the man whose elective system means freedom for them and opportunity. . . .

So he will always stand out before them, before the college youth as before the nation: a guide in democracy.

7

The Printer and the Riddle

HENRY GEORGE

*The arch-rebel, Thomas Jefferson, once said: "The
earth is given as a common stock for men to labor and
live on." He hoped America would be a nation of
people more or less equal in wealth. In a land of mil-
lionaires and beggars, he felt, democracy dies out.*

*Yet as the wealth of the country grew, so did its
poverty. Here was HENRY GEORGE'S riddle, and a disease at the heart of democracy. How explain it, how
cure it?*

THE PRINTER AND THE RIDDLE

I

THE riddle first challenged him when he was a boy of eighteen. He had a job then in a printing house in Philadelphia, where he was born. As the youngest typesetter in the house he liked to goad the older men into debates. He used to stand at the case and raise all sorts of questions in politics, religion, travel — culled from his reading the night before.

They were talking of hard times one day, and an elderly printer remarked that wages were much higher in the United States than anywhere in Europe. "That's because the United States is young," he explained. "When a land gets old, like Europe, people find it hard to make a living there. Wages sink so low. Look at us in America: Wages are higher in California than in New York. That's because California is younger."

"But why?" asked Henry George. "Why should the age of a country affect the pay envelope? Don't the people do the same amount of work whatever the age of their country?"

The elderly printer did not know.

"The older the country, the richer," persisted the young man. "I should think its wages would be higher."

"But they aren't."

And that was the riddle that lodged in Henry George's mind.

It came up again for an answer shortly after when he sat on the deck of a schooner in the Pacific Ocean, bound for the Fraser River in British Columbia. He had worked his passage out to California, in search of the higher wages of the new land. San Francisco was then a city of shanties stuck to sides of a sheaf of hills, its streets restless with fortune hunters. There was gold in the hills. But when Henry George arrived in 1858, the best "claims" had already been located, and the look in the eyes of the fortune hunters grew day by day hungrier. He himself had taken odd jobs at his trade of printing, meanwhile sharing the golden dreams of his neighbors. Suddenly the news broke out of the discovery of placer mines on the banks of the Fraser River. The land was still untenanted and waiting to be staked out. At once the docks of San Francisco were crowded with emigrants, Henry George among them.

On the deck of the schooner, which took each

man to his own nugget, the miners exchanged stories of lucky strikes, of how this or that prospector had dug and washed dirt for months without scraping together enough "dust" to buy a fried egg, and how one day — and, well, how he was back home now with the world in his pocket. Every cheek flushed. They spoke of California, how it had lured people from every corner of the world, even China.

"There's the trouble," said one of the miners. "The Chinese should be kept out."

"They don't do us any harm," objected Henry George. "They work the cheap diggings. We don't care to work them."

"They do no harm now," admitted the miner. "But wages will not always be as high as they are to-day in California. As the country grows, wages will come down, and some day we shall be glad to get those diggings that the Chinamen are now working."

Again the ominous riddle!

Later he encountered it on another turn in the road of Western progress. Plans were in the air to lay down a railroad overland between St. Joseph, Missouri, and Sacramento, linking the Far West to the East. In the streets of San Francisco men spoke of the coming of the railroad as the priests in the mission spoke of the millennium. The railroad would bring prosperity to the West.

"Yet what good will it bring men like me, hired hands?" wondered Henry George.

He had had no luck in the gold hunt, had come back dead broke to his old job of setting type. He saw no hope in further prospecting. All the good diggings had been staked out, every river bed and bank worked over, and only the barren ones left. The new prospectors turned to the dry diggings in ravines, on hillsides. They bored wells, sank shafts into the earth, shot columns of water against the hillside, and were lucky if they washed out enough "pay dirt" for a day's wages. Rumor whispered of the good pay dirt yonder, here, there. But the sun had set for the adventurer prowling with his shovel, pick and pan.

The gold fever had gone from the blood of young Henry George and left him depressed. He had been led on by a mirage of wealth, and found himself instead working long and hard for bare sustenance.

"How I long for the Golden Age," he wrote to the folks back home, "when the poorest will have a chance to use all his God-given faculties, and not be forced to drudge away the best part of his time. . . . Sometimes I feel sick of the fierce struggle of our high civilized life."

He worked so much of the day that he had no time or energy left for reading in the evening. He wore his clothes until they were rags. He economized in every way, yet he hadn't enough to meet his board bill. Times were bitter. In Sacramento the first shovelful of earth was dug for the railroad which was to join the East to the West and, so people said, bring good times. Henry George was doubtful. Why was it that the wealthier a country became, the poorer its people? Sphinx-like, the riddle taunted him.

Times grew even worse for him. He had married, and with work scarce and a family to support, he was frantic. The day his second baby was born, he had no money to buy food. He went into the street and walked along slowly, eyeing every passer. At last he picked his man, stopped him and spoke in a firm tone.

"I need five dollars. Will you let me have it?"

The man looked at him. "What do you want it for?"

"My wife is ill. I have nothing to give her to eat."

The stranger hesitated, then reached into his pocket.

"What would I have done," wondered Henry George afterward, "had he refused? I was desperate." He saw that poverty breeds criminals as well as beggars. That was why the riddle must be answered. "Yes," he thought. "The railroad will bring us wealth. Those who have, will have more; but the average person will be poorer. San

159

Francisco will build its fine mansions; but along with them the slum will arise, the almshouse and the jail."

The riddle that stalked him threw him its last and fiercest challenge in the city of New York. Times had improved for him; he was now an editor of a San Francisco newspaper which had sent him East on business. New York fascinated him. He saw avenues lined with mansions, and people in coaches. But when he turned his head, he seemed to behold the skeleton beneath this fair complexion of things: homes worse than shacks in the hills, people gaunt and weary. He saw small dogs fed and housed, and little children in want. He saw men and women swathed luxuriously, and others without the daily crust of bread.

"And yet," he thought, "there is enough wealth here for the needs of all."

When he was a boy of sixteen he had gone to sea. He had sailed up the Ganges in India, thrilled to be in the land of soft airs and dreamy luxury. At least so it was described in books. But the real India before him was a bitter disappointment. He saw the princely luxury of a few, saw jewels blaze in the trappings of elephants. But most human life he saw groveling in the dirt.

Now New York impressed him the same way.

His yearning for the sea had been inspired by the tales he had read of missionaries who had gone

abroad to spread Light and Truth among the be-
nighted people of the earth.

Now he longed to become a missionary among
his own people, to teach them to stamp out the
disease of poverty.

Pity roused him to confront the riddle once for
all time. "This riddle has its root somewhere.
Wealth and want spring from the same seed," he
believed. This seed he must find. Then, taking humanity by the hand, he would lead them to it,
that they might destroy it. Although he had quit
school before his fourteenth birthday, he had never
stopped studying. Now he assigned to himself the
problem: Why do a few people have so much, and
most people so little?

A man of thirty, small and erect, with a full
sandy beard and alert blue eyes, had undertaken
to answer the riddle of the ages.

II

One afternoon, not long after his return to San
Francisco, he took his horse for a gallop in the
country. The clear stretch of wild land refreshed
him; the jolting of his mount threw off him the
cares of the day. Far in the distance he seemed to
see a row of ties and poles bobbing past: the
railroad was finished. The ground beneath his

161

mustang's hoofs was wild, but no longer free. It belonged to someone now. Everyone was in a rush to buy land. The railroad, people said, would raise its value. Buy land and hold it, they advised.

The mustang was panting and his rider drew in the reins. As they halted, a teamster happened along, and he, too, stopped.

"What's land worth around here?" asked Henry George.

The teamster pointed to some cows grazing in the distance. "That man wants a thousand dollars an acre."

Something clicked in the mind of Henry George, like a door opening wide. He was dazed with the flood of light that streamed in over him, dazed with the sight of the thing he had been looking for: the answer to the riddle.

Home he charged. He had to be alone to work it out. He had hold of the bare idea. That man who wanted one thousand dollars an acre, for his land — what had he done to earn that money? Nothing: he was just shrewd enough to foresee that more and more people would settle around his land. Land is the one thing you cannot create. Those people would need his land; he could raise the price of it.

"That is why," thought Henry George trembling with excitement, "that is why the more our community grows, the more wealth we are forced to

162

hand over to landlords. The people remain poor but the few landlords grow richer."

He sat down at his table to publish the thought. There flashed into his mind the image of the four men who built the railroad. As though in gratitude, the Government had given away to these men more than twenty-five thousand acres of the people's ground for each mile of railroad they had built. Few people cared. The vast empty territory of the West seemed worthless. Yet that gift had made the four men multimillionaires. . . .

It was wrong to give away the people's land, he wrote. True, just then, we had more land than we could use. That was because America was young. Land was still cheap; on the frontier, even free. His free land on the frontier made the American independent. He worked for nobody unless he was well paid for his work. He was cheerful and confident, because he was independent. For the same reason he was hospitable to strangers, to the downtrodden foreigner. He could afford to be. God's earth was plentiful.

But land had its end, Henry George pointed out. At the rate it was being fenced in, another twenty years would see the end of America's free ground. Already there were men who owned more land than a horse could gallop over in a day. One day we, the people, would need that land, and would have to pay tribute for it to the lord of the domain:

rent to the landlord. We would have to give him a share of the crops we raised, or a share of our wages, just for the privilege of building our house on it. And as the country grew, the landlord's share of our labor would grow larger until we should become no better than his slaves. Such was already the case in Europe, and so it was developing in the East. Thus, when people said that wages were low in the old countries, they meant that the landlords there took away a high share of the wealth produced. That was the answer to the riddle.

"But what of it!" he could hear the objection come from outside his window. "This is the country of opportunity. One man is the owner of a factory, another of a shop, and a third man owns a piece of land. Business is business."

Henry George was ready with his reply: "Oh, no. There's a difference. The landlord did not earn his profit. He did no work. He merely waited until his land was needed by other people. The community that came to his land created its value. That value belongs by right to the community, to all the people."

How can they get it?

"It's all very well to find fault," went on the voice of objection. "But if there's nothing to be done about it, you're wasting time."

"We must do something," warned Henry George.

"Otherwise the very ground which nourishes and shelters us, as vital to us as air, will be monopolized by a few men. Those few will own and rule us. And then democracy will perish."

"What would you have done?"

"One step only can safeguard us and our children: We must claim what is ours, every cent of ground-rent."

"What would happen if we so taxed the landlord?"

"It would no longer pay him to hold on to his acres. Land would become cheap. Settlements of people would flourish everywhere. The worker could reap the full harvest of his work. No longer would children starve in the streets of New York, to provide the princes of the Avenue with splendor. All our people could then live in ease and freedom. Through that single tax on land, democracy would be saved."

This was the powerful thought with which Henry George would abolish poverty. It kept whirling in his mind, and developing, and upon it his spirit soared. He saw the planet Earth sailing through space, a well-provisioned ship. But it seemed whenever a quantity of food was drawn up out of the hatches a few officers stepped forward and laid hands on it. The rest of the crew got only the leavings.

If he could conjure up ghosts, he would summon old Ben Franklin, the man of perfect common sense, and say to him: "The world has changed miraculously since your day. Hear the throb of our engines. Those are the slaves of our lamp. They can turn out a case of shoes in less time than one of your cobblers takes to put on a sole. They can spin cotton into cloth almost without the lift of a human finger. They can harvest our crops and build our houses."

He predicted the comment of the old sage: —

"Oh, to be alive now! For with plenty for everyone, life must be beautiful; your hearts pure of envy and greed; your bodies radiant; your minds in search of perfection. Pray, what means that terrifying roar?"

"That is the cry of masses of men out of work."

"Did you not say that your engines — "

"Yes, but those engines belong to few."

"Let the men without work do as we did. Let them go into the wilderness."

"That, too, belongs to a few."

Poor Richard would understand. "Then I seem to see a land of beggars and criminals; a land poorer than in my day; a land of discontent and misery." And without a trace of regret, the shade would vanish.

For three years Henry George spent his happiest hours in his room on First Street, San Francisco, in the company of his figures and his visions. His children, stealing past, saw him bent over his table in the center of the room overlooking the Bay, his cheeks glowing and his pen gliding over the paper. During the night, sometimes, when the tide beat strongly against the docks, they awoke and there in the hall lay a yellow beam thrown by their father's lamp. At dawn the beam had paled, but not gone out. A little more of their father's plan for a better world had been drawn.

They tiptoed into his room, perhaps, when he went walking, or down to the newspaper office where he sometimes worked. They looked with awe at the sermon paper neatly piled on the table; at the bold letters written in blue ink. The words were lofty and melodious, but hard. Even the title was hard: "Progress and Poverty." But now and then little stories seemed to break out over the page. There was one about a pioneer driving his wagon over a grassy plain.

The poor fellow is looking for a home. He notices that around him the soil is rich. He hears the rustle of game, and sees trout flashing in the stream. He may as well build his cabin right there, he thinks. The only trouble with the place is that there are no people near by. He and his family have to do everything for themselves — build their own house, kill their own food, make their own

167

clothes. They are very poor, they have only food and shelter.

But presently another wagon rolls over the plain, another pioneer. He, too, can settle anywhere, but, since it is better for him to have a neighbor, he builds his house next to the first pioneer's. Pretty soon others arrive. The plain rings with pleasant sounds, and the men help one another in labor. Life is richer for everyone. Instead of each man's building his own wagon, or making his own shoes, one of them sets up a shop and builds all the wagons of the settlement, or makes all the shoes. Instead of everybody's journeying to town to sell his corn and buy his utensils, one man only need go back and forth; he opens a store. Pooling together, they hire a teacher. As the seasons roll over the little village, there are husking bees, apple parings, quilting parties.

But what happens to our hero, the first pioneer? It seems that someone says to him: "You've built a barn and a house. You've put up fences and planted an orchard. Now I'll pay you all that it cost you and I'll pay you for your labor, too. You don't care about the land itself, do you? Beyond the village there's just as fertile land you can have for nothing."

Our hero laughs loudly. Why, his land is next to the general store; a doctor has moved across the road; the schoolhouse is right there. He wouldn't take less than fifty dollars an acre for his land.

The village grows into a good-sized town. The spot our hero had once found so wild and lonely teems with a thousand people. All kinds of shops have come to it. A railroad puffs by. Our hero's land is worth one thousand dollars an acre. In time, when the town has grown into a city, an acre may be worth ten thousand dollars. Our hero, or his children, suddenly find themselves rich. And they have done nothing but sit on their acres. To the end of time other people, more and more of them, will have to work for his children's children. . . .

The only point the George children could make of this story was that somehow our hero wasn't a hero at all; he was really a sort of villain, because he made people pay him for nothing he had done.

Perhaps the children overheard their father discuss "Progress and Poverty" with his friends. . . .

"We must make land the property of all," argued Henry George.

"You mean to divide up all the land equally?" asked his critics. "You couldn't do that."

"That is not what I mean," replied George. "Let the world carry on exactly as it does to-day. I would merely have our Government take all ground-rent."

His critics had a serious objection. "Yes, perhaps the world would then be a better place to live in.

But would it be fair to take away all the ground-rent from people who paid money for it? Your first pioneers are no more. They have sold their land. Is it right to punish the people who bought it?"

"Was it right to take the slaves away from people who bought them?" retorted Henry George. "Suppose Captain Kidd, the pirate, had robbed your grandfather of a fortune. Now suppose that Kidd's grandson has the fortune which you would have had. The law says: 'Young Mr. Kidd never harmed you. You must let bygones be bygones.' Is that fair? Well, our early pioneers were land pirates, although innocent ones. They took for themselves the increasing value of the land, even though they had not earned it. Unearned increment of land belongs to all of us. Let us claim it."

The children wished they could hear more about the pirates — "unearned increment" were such hard words. But they liked to listen to their father when he spoke, with a faraway look as though fixed on some vision outside the room, about the new world his single tax on land would make. In that world nobody could be poor. In that world their father would not have had to pawn his watch to pay the grocer. Young boys would not have to go to work, like Junior; they could continue their schooling. Nobody would be out of work, and no workers would ever need to go on a strike because their wages would be high enough. Everybody then could be honest, and really have what Thomas Jefferson said he was entitled to have: life, liberty, and the pursuit of happiness. At present, as their father said, Americans had the right to vote but not to work. They had the ballot but no bread, and there was starvation and misery throughout the land of the free and equal. . . .

One night in the spring of 1879 the gleam of light lay outside Henry George's room, as usual. Within, shortly before dawn rose out of the bay, Henry George laid down his pen. He had just written: "Beauty still lies imprisoned, and iron wheels go over the good and true and beautiful that might spring from human lives."

It was almost the last sentence of the book, "Progress and Poverty," and the face of the author was wet with tears. He was about to send into the world the vision that lived in his brain. What would the world say?

III

At first the world said little, and Henry George at the age of forty-two found himself with his book under his arm in New York, poor and unknown, in search of a job. But suddenly the spotlight of fame turned upon him. Throughout the country workingmen, in the midst of bitter strikes for wages and jobs, became aware of an eloquent voice speaking for them in the pages of a book called "Progress and Poverty." They hailed the book as a prophecy and demanded ever more copies of it. They called for the author, and Henry George went on tour, lecturing before crowds of people in the United States and Canada. His fiery presence branding his message into their hearts.

Who could answer him? Could anyone deny the pinched faces in the streets of a big city? No one with a heart in his body could fail to be moved by the squalor and the distress in the tenements of New York or the slums of Chicago. No one who had seen the figures of men and women shuffling aimlessly outside a factory, like discards of flesh and blood, could resist joining Henry George in pleading for those who were racked with poverty and uncertainty.

There were thoughtful people who agreed with Henry George that democracy would die unless something were done to elevate the masses of men, but who doubted whether his plan of a single tax on land was the right plan. With those people Henry George was always willing to debate. But there were others who raised a hue and cry against him, who shook their fists at him and called him "Robber! Revolutionist! Anarchist!" — their fists flashing with diamonds. Many hesitant people, judging Henry George by his enemies, enlisted in his cause.

Abroad his fame was more intense than at home. He got his first invitation to cross the sea from Ireland, where the suffering of the poor was more pitiable than anywhere else in Great Britain. After his visit his name became Irish household words. But honor of him spread through all the British Isles. Next to the Prime Minister, he was the most talked-of person; and groups of men were organized to act on his plan. The great scientist, Alfred Russel Wallace, said that in his opinion "Progress and Poverty" was the most important book of the century.

When he returned to America, he was greeted by huge throngs of workingmen to whom he lectured at Cooper Union, in New York. Shortly after, it happened that an election for the office of Mayor was facing the city. The labor unions, deciding to put up a candidate of their own, were unanimous on only one man, Henry George, and they appealed to him to accept their nomination. The author of "Progress and Poverty," just then in great demand as lecturer and writer, was reluctant to enter politics. But a petition of 30,000 people touched him and he consented to run.

He almost won, too, which fact frightened the wits out of some people — those whom it profited to believe Henry George a highwayman from the

173

West. Nearly 70,000 people voted for him. As they put their mark after his name on the ballot, what did those people signify? They seemed to say: "In a world as rich as ours, poverty is absurd. It is not nature's, it is man's fault. Men have divided up their wealth stupidly and selfishly. We must re-divide it more wisely and more justly. Democracy, which decrees freedom for every man, is the most beautiful of ideals. But no man is free when he is as poor as millions of us are, for he is bound by hunger, by all his pangs and those of his family. From those he must be freed."

This was the basis of Henry George's politics. "It is not the end of the campaign," he said after Election Day. "We have fought the first skirmish."

His next move was to start a weekly newspaper, the *Standard*, in which he broadcast his protest against progress with poverty, and the *Standard* gave rise to an Anti-Poverty Society. Meanwhile his world popularity was growing and in 1890 came his third call abroad, this time to the South Sea Islands continent, Australia and New Zealand. Once he had visited Australia, with a ship's crew when he was sixteen. Now, at the age of fifty-one, he came as one of Australia's most celebrated men. Whenever he went on the island continent he was the guest of honor of Single-Tax and Anti-Poverty Societies. To this day, although his principles of the land tax are practised in various parts of the

world, it flourishes best throughout Australia and
New Zealand. When he returned to New York,
however, his honor at home was rival to that
abroad. He found in progress a national convention
of "single-tax" men. He heard himself dubbed
"Saint George."

In June 1897, the labor unions again asked him
to run for the office of Mayor of New York. This
time, it was felt, the banner of Saint George could
be raised on the City Hall. There was one fear —
on the score of Henry George's health. He was sick
from overwork. His face was ashen, his body thin.
The physician forbade his taking part in the campaign.

"Tell me," Henry George asked the doctor. "If
I accept, what is the worst that can happen to
me?"

"Since you ask," answered the doctor, "you have
a right to be told. It will most probably prove
fatal."

"You mean it may kill me?"

"Yes."

The patient shrugged. "I've got to die. How can
I die better than by serving humanity?"

He thought of the line of men standing on cold
nights outside a Broadway bakeshop where the
stale, unsold loaves of bread were given away. He
would run.

He had to be helped to the platform of Cooper

Union where, before the throng of workingmen, he accepted their nomination.

"You ask me to raise the standard again . . ." he said in a weak voice, "for that great cause; to stand as Jefferson stood. . . . I accept."

Thomas Jefferson had once said: "The earth belongs to the living and not to the dead. The earth is given as a common stock for men to labor and live on." Therefore, Henry George's party became "The Party of Thomas Jefferson."

His doctor was right; the strenuous campaign proved too much for him, and on the eve of the election he took his seat among the immortals by the side of Thomas Jefferson.

"He was a tribune of the people," agreed the newspapers the next day, "poor for their sake when he might have been rich. All his life long he spoke, and wrote, and thought, and prayed, and dreamed of one thing only — the cause of the plain people. He died as he lived, striking at the enemies of the people. . . . He was a thinker whose work belongs to the world's literature. His death has carried mourning into every civilized country on the globe."

But Henry George has written his own portrait in the pages of "Progress and Poverty." He speaks of his ideal man: —

"He turns his back upon the feast . . . he leaves it to others to accumulate wealth . . . to bask themselves in the warm sunshine. . . . He works for those he never saw and never can see. . . . He toils in the advance where it is cold, and there is little cheer from men, and the stones are sharp and the brambles thick. Into higher, grander spheres . . ."

. . . Where Henry George comes at last, and stands fixed among the traditions of America.

8

Judge Holmes and the Constitution

In the heaven provided for democracy's faithful, the shade of Henry George may have startled the shade of Thomas Jefferson with the story of changes in America since 1776. Thomas Jefferson had wished a different fate for his country.

Among the living as well were mourners for the old days. But the renowned MR. JUSTICE HOLMES *was stoical.*

"Much that we hold dear must be done away with," he said.

Life goes on. New generations, new needs. The Needy clamor at the doors of the Satisfied. The latter are indignant.

"Our rights!" they cry.

"Our needs!"

In the ancient days of absolute monarchs, the strain of this conflict cracked the kingdom. But in a democracy the Satisfied take shelter in the law. And the Needy try to change the law. There is then a hasty retreat to the ramparts of democracy, — the Constitution, — and the black-robed Judges are called in.

Let us summon JUDGE HOLMES.

JUDGE HOLMES AND THE
CONSTITUTION

I

SCANNING the sea of events recorded in his newspaper, the average man is usually attracted by the rolling wave of the moment. Seldom does he care anything about the deep currents that imperceptibly govern his life. So in the summer of 1902 he doubtless failed to take notice of a ripple in the shifting current of events. "Supreme Court Justice Retires." One cannot blame the average citizen for giving that news scant thought. The Supreme Court of the United States is the one governmental area from which he is excluded. The founders of the Republic had so intended. Distrusting him, they had removed the highest court of the land from the reach of his ballot.

"The President," they provided in the Constitution, "shall nominate and by and with the advice and consent of the Senate shall appoint judges of the Supreme Court. . . . The judges shall hold their offices during good behavior. . . ."

The burden of filling the seat left vacant rested, then, largely in the hands of President Theodore Roosevelt. Never was the President's responsibility greater. The man he looked for was to sit on the bench of perhaps the most imposing court of law in the world. He, together with his eight colleagues, was sometimes more powerful than the President, the Congress, or the people themselves. He could on occasions overrule all their acts, and he was answerable to none.

Curious anomaly in a democracy! Once the king was the court of final appeal. Now, like a surviving vestige of monarchy, it is the Supreme Court. Was it for this that America won her freedom from king? When they revolted from Great Britain, the Thirteen States of North America agreed in their Articles of Confederation that the Congress was the Supreme Court of the land. But they really wanted no Supreme Court at all. They saw to it that Congress should be unable to enforce its acts.

"What!" exclaimed the citizens of each state, "has our state won its independence from a Parliament, only to be subjected to a Congress?"

On those terms no union was possible, and the leaders of the states convened in 1787 to draw up the Constitution of the United States and grudgingly to surrender, for the sake of the union, some of their independence. But, still suspicious of Congress, of the President, of each other, of the common people, of the next generation, they invented a Supreme Court to protect themselves from their own tyranny.

From the decisions of the Supreme Court, however, there can be no protection under the Constitution. That was why, in appointing a new Supreme Court justice, the responsibility of President Theodore Roosevelt was so heavy. The man he looked for must be upright, learned, wise, and devoted to the spirit of his country; for without such qualities a justice of the Supreme Court was a tyrant. Who was that man?

Prominent Americans awaited the results of the search anxiously. The nation was growing and changing. The factory was displacing the farm; the city was moving out into the country. Miraculous inventions and swarms of immigrants were revising American life and creating problems unimaginable when the law of the land was born, and the solution of those problems affected the history of the country. The President was in search of a history-maker. The average citizen took little interest in the names before the president. He took little interest in the Supreme Court or the Constitution. To him they were as remote as the constellation of fixed stars over his house. He knew about them, but they did not touch him. He could recite mechanically: "We, the people of the United States, in order to form a more perfect union . . ." and

183

there he would break down, the rest swept from his memory together with other lessons of the schoolmaster's rod.

Yet here and there a citizen in the crowd realized that the President's choice did touch him. If he was a baker living in the State of New York, for instance, he must have been excited. His State Legislature had enacted a law limiting his working day to ten hours. A baking company defied the law on the ground that it was unconstitutional, and was carrying the fight to the Supreme Court. The bakers of New York were therefore concerned in the President's decision. So were the railroad men everywhere in the country. A law of Congress prohibited railroad companies from discharging employees who were members of a union. The railroads defied the law, contending it was unconstitutional. Every worker in the country was concerned in the identity of the new Supreme Court justice. A group of bankers were about to fight the Government, in the Supreme Court; the farmers of Texas, a railroad company. Even the school children of Massachusetts had a stake in the new justice. On the decision of the Supreme Court depended whether they were to pay half fare or full fare on their ride to school.

Baker, trainman, banker, union member, student, farmer — every citizen was affected when in December, 1902, the new justice of the Supreme

Court took his seat. The lawyer preparing to plead his case before the Supreme Court stopped work on his brief to wonder: "Who is he? What is his character, his station in life? How does he look at the law? What treatment can we expect from him?"

II

His name was Oliver Wendell Holmes, a name made illustrious already by his father, a writer and physician.

"Last evening between eight and nine," Dr. Holmes wrote on March 10, 1841, "there appeared at my house a little individual who may be hereafter addressed as —— Holmes, Esq., or the Hon. —— Holmes, M.C., or His Excellency — Holmes, President, etc., etc., but who for the present is content with scratching his face and sucking his right forefinger."

The son and namesake of Oliver Wendell Holmes started out indeed as close to the summit of success as wealth and social standing could bring him. The most elegant mansions of Boston were open to him. At Harvard, and in the company of his father, he became intimate with the brilliant minds of the country. Emerson, Lowell, Longfellow, and others as famous, were frequently his table companions. . . . "A blueblood, a born aristocrat," thinks the corporation lawyer with satisfaction. "He will appreciate our side of the case."

At twenty, young "Wendell" Holmes, graduate of Harvard and poet of his class, thought to devote himself to the retired life of a scholar. By nature he was studious, and as a student had become interested in philosophy. At that instant the Civil War burst like a bomb under his peaceful dreams. Now Wendell Holmes could be philosophical, even in youth, about all questions save one: slavery. And so he put a marker in his open volume of Plato, got himself a sword, a blue uniform, and a company of men, and the tall, spare student in search of wisdom became the lieutenant in search of death. At Ball's Bluff a rebel bullet went neatly through his body, but made neither corpse nor civilian of him, but a captain. At Antietam a ball pierced his neck. He hurried through this disability in time to rejoin his company at Chancellorsville and meet the piece of shrapnel that shattered his heel. In all he was wounded five times. Doubtless Fate had its sign on him: *Preserved for Immortality*. . . . "He is then an idealist," observes the lawyer opposing the corporation. "He would sacrifice himself to a humane cause. A patriot, he is devoted to the welfare of his country. That is encouraging to our side of the case."

The war over, young Holmes faced the question

of his future. The tumult and smoke of the battle had left him discontented with the inaction of a scholar's life. He did not wish to withdraw from the world, but neither did he wish to become a puppet of the world. One career seemed to combine the excitement of the battle with the peace of the study, and that was the law. He enrolled, therefore, in the Harvard Law School and in 1867 was admitted to the bar.

Yet the lamp in his study had cast upon him an undeniable charm; within the circle of its light he was happier than among the shadows of legal practice. He practiced very little, in fact. Although he worked indefatigably, it was as an instructor of Constitutional Law in Harvard and as the editor of the *American Law Journal* — as a scholar of the law. . . . "I must know his views on the law," thinks the attorney about to plead before Justice Holmes. He would be wise first to take down from his bookshelf a famous volume called: "The Common Law," by O. W. Holmes, Jr. The book is one of the greatest in its line, written in 1880 when the author was still a teacher of the law.

When he has turned the last page of "The Common Law," the lawyer very likely reconsiders his brief. He may find, for instance, that to support his claim he has relied too heavily on some ancient rule of law. "A precedent," he calls it when he unearths the opinion of a judge dead one hundred or five hundred years ago. Usually the lawyer is happy to uncover a precedent for his case. The mere sanction of the past is awesome before the court.

"That is all very well," teaches Justice Holmes. "But it is revolting to have no better reason for a rule of law than that it was laid down in the time of Henry IV."

Not that he scorns the past. Quite the contrary. But he knows too much about the past to follow it blindly. For instance, he considers this case. A baker's man, driving his master's cart to deliver hot rolls one morning, runs another man down. The master has to pay for the injury.

"But why?" asks the innocent baker.

"You are to blame," answers his lawyer, "for hiring a careless man. That is an ancient rule of law."

"But I chose the man carefully," insists the baker.

"That is no excuse. You sent the man to deliver the rolls. You can pay for the damage."

The baker is not satisfied. Neither is Oliver Wendell Holmes. He investigates the respectable "ancient rule of law." Beyond the distant horizons of time, he finds its most remote ancestor a savage law of vengeance. He traces it among the Hebrew tribes encamped in the wilderness of Sinai, when it decrees: "If an ox gore a man or a woman, that they die: then the ox shall be surely stoned, and

188

his flesh shall not be eaten; but the owner of the ox shall be quit." He comes upon it amid the Greeks of Plato's time, where it decrees that a stone that kills a man is to be banished. "And if a man commits suicide, bury the hand that struck the blow afar from its body." And if a slave wounded a man he was to be given up to the man as damages.

That would have been the fate of the baker's man as revenge for his crime, whereas now the blameless baker himself must expiate.

"Oh, why," may the poor fellow wail, "did they change such excellent laws!"

Oliver Wendell Holmes tracks it down among the Romans. He delves in the forests of time and picks up the trail of the law of vengeance among the German tribes. He pursues it across the channel and finds it living under King Alfred. "If a neat wound a man, let the neat be delivered up." But by this time the "ancient rule of law" has changed its form. The owner of the miscreant thing or creature may redeem it with money. The rule of law has adapted itself to more civilized conditions, and centuries later it takes on its most modern form which makes the baker liable for the act of his servant.

"Laws are like living creatures," believed Justice Holmes. "Both change their forms to meet new needs." In arctic climes, animal life develops fur, and adopts habits suitable to the climate; in tropical climes his form and habits are different. The living creature changes when life demands, or perishes. So with laws. Darwin's theory of evolution applies to both.

Before reading "The Common Law," the lawyer may have seen in the law the vision of a lovely statue of a woman, blindfolded and holding up the scales of justice. From Holmes he learns that the law is more like a creature of flesh and blood, dressed in the serviceable garments of a housekeeper, and carrying a market basket.

"The law is society's means of getting what it needs," demonstrated Oliver Wendell Holmes.

Throughout the English-speaking world "The Common Law" was hailed as one of the greatest legal works of the century, and was translated into German, French, and Italian. Shortly after its publication, it happened that a judge of the Supreme Court of Massachusetts retired, and the Governor could think of no one more fitting to fill the vacancy than the author of "The Common Law."

"To think of it!" exclaimed Oliver Wendell Holmes, father. "My little boy a judge, and able to send me to jail if I don't behave myself!"

And seventeen years later, in 1899, Justice Holmes became Chief Justice of the Supreme Court of Massachusetts. His conspicuous position alone entitled him to the regard of the President when in 1902 he cast about for a new justice of the Supreme Court of the land.

The lawyer about to plead before the Supreme Court wants to know Holmes's record as a judge. That he can discover by browsing through the opinions of the Massachusetts Supreme Court. From at least one great case, he gathers what to expect.

During a labor strike, an employer appealed to the court for an injunction forbidding the labor unions to picket his shop. The Massachusetts Supreme Court consists of seven judges. Five of the the seven judges opined that the employer was in the right.

"Pickets are damaging to business," argued the five judges.

"They use no force," objected Holmes.

"No, but they interfere with the man's business nevertheless."

"So do his competitors," retorted Holmes.

"Injunction granted," voted the majority.

Holmes dissented. "Many people," he remarked, "have believed strikes wicked. But we must not stand in the path of progress. Industrial progress has brought about great combinations of capital. We have benefited thereby. And what capital has a right to do, so has labor. Labor ought to unite, and does; and as long as labor unions use peaceful

191

means they should have the sanction of the law."

All his opinions delivered from the bench of the Massachusetts' Supreme Court were in line with his new and bold belief that the principles of justice must be interpreted to fit the changing needs of society. It was not the law, he confessed, that counts most in a courtroom; it was the judge's private views.

Corporation executives frowned upon Judge Holmes's social views. For one thing his sympathy with labor was not encouraging to them. But that was just what President Theodore Roosevelt liked about him. And that was why he appointed Judge Oliver Wendell Holmes to the bench of the greatest court of law in the world.

III

"Oyez! Oyez! Oyez! All persons having business before the honorable judges of the Supreme Court of the United States are admonished to draw near and give their attention, for the court is now sitting. God save the United States and this honorable court."

The frock-coated crier has performed the ritual, the audience find seats, and the wheels of the law begin to turn. Lawyers step forward, their papers drawn; briefs, evidence, and other solemn paraphernalia. Behind a long table sit the nine justices, masked in robes of black. The curious spectator finds names from the world of men to apply to each of the judicial visages.

Harlan — Peckham — White — and there is Holmes, who listens, erect and intent. The curved sweep of his mustachios and the firm set of his shoulders mark the military man. But the deep eyes and the high brow belong to the scholar. Listening to the argument of the learned counsel, the Justice is as taut as a tiger about to leap, as ominous as a storm about to break. Suddenly he flings a question to the speaker; again, and another; and he is satisfied. The learned counsel picks up the broken thread of his speech, but Holmes has stopped listening. He reads over the briefs, calls the page to bring him the court opinions cited by counsel. Before the speaker has ended his convincing argument, Justice Holmes is ready with his opinion.

Most of the time the case is of little moment. Now and then the intelligent eyes of the country are on the Supreme Court, as they were in 1904 when the court heard Lochner *v.* New York.

The story of the case is simple. It has to do with bakers. The Legislature of New York felt that a baker's hours of work were too long, both for the baker and for the people who ate his bread. It

193

enacted a law, therefore, prohibiting his working for more than ten hours a day.

"This law is an outrage!" exclaimed the officials of a baking company in Utica. "We will pay no attention to it."

"Then pay the fine provided for violation of the law," ordered the inspector.

The company paid. The fine was cheaper than hiring more men. Again the inspector came around, and again he laid the fine. This time the company protested and its lawyers went to court. The law was unfair, they contended. They entrenched behind the Fourteenth Amendment to the Constitution.

". . . Nor shall any State deprive any person of life, liberty, or property, without due process of law; nor deny to any person . . . the equal protection of the laws."

This amendment had been ratified right after the Civil War, its purpose being to protect the freed Negroes in the South. Now the baking company found it of advantage.

"The ten-hour law," their lawyers attacked, "deprives us of property. It discriminates against baking companies, and so denies them the equal protection of the laws. It is therefore unconstitutional."

The case landed at last in the Supreme Court of the United States. When the attorneys had

194

finished their arguments, the nine justices retired to thrash the matter out privately, and without black robes. The Chief Justice summed up the arguments of either side, and put the question: Was the ten-hour baker's law unconstitutional?

"Yes," said one, "it is. The right to buy and sell is one of the liberties hinted at in the Fourteenth Amendment."

"No," said another, "it is not. The states have reserved the right to protect the health of their citizens."

A collision of rights! How decide?

"Good bread does not depend on whether a baker works ten hours or twelve hours a day."

"The people of New York seem to think it does," observed Mr. Justice Holmes. "And that is enough for us."

"No," decided a majority of five. "It is not enough. The people of New York have enacted a meddlesome law. It is shocking," they added, "how such unwise laws are spreading throughout the country."

"That is the people's affair, not ours," said Mr. Justice Holmes. "The Constitution is no strait jacket around the will of the people. As for interfering with the liberty of the baking company, every law interferes with somebody. We judges may not like this law or that, but unless the Constitution expressly forbids it, we should refer to the will of the people."

With that, Oliver Wendell Holmes announced a new principle of law in America. It became known that he disliked frustrating acts of the people by decreeing them unconstitutional. The danger was, he felt, that the judges of the Supreme Court might play the part of tyrants.

"Save the laws of the people," he warned his colleagues. "It is our duty. Don't use the broad words of our Constitution to hamper democracy. They are there to protect it."

He had numerous occasions to repeat the warning.

"Oyez! Oyez! Oyez! . . . the court is now sitting. God save the United States and this honorable court."

In 1898, after a serious railroad labor strike in Chicago, Congress passed the Erdman Act. One section of the Act prohibited railroad companies from discharging an employee solely because he belonged to a union. That was why, in 1907, on the docket of the Supreme Court appeared the case of Adair *v.* United States. A railroad corporation had discharged a fireman because he would not give up his union card. As usual, the battle was waged on the broad ground of the Constitution. The corporation barricaded itself behind the Fifth Amendment.

The first ten amendments, known as the Bill of

Rights, were originally put down as the standing guard of liberty. In 1787, Thomas Jefferson, who was in Paris when the Constitution was drafted, wrote to his friend James Madison approving the Constitution. But, he criticized, there was no Bill of Rights; he would like to see plainly stated everyone's right to his religion, to free speech, to trial by jury, and to a few other essentials of democracy. In this criticism Jefferson had popular support, for most people feared that their hard-won liberties might later be trodden under unless planted clearly in the Constitution. At once, therefore, ten amendments were added to the new Constitution. The Fifth provides that no person shall be deprived of life, liberty, or property "without due process of law" — which means unjustly. This amendment is the stock defense against an Act of Congress, as its descendant, the Fourteenth Amendment, is the stock defense against an act of a State Legislature.

Resisting the attack on the Erdman Act, the Government countered with the power of Congress "to regulate commerce along the several states." This, in fact, was the foremost duty of Congress. In the days immediately after the Revolution, each state then being a law unto itself, merchants were so hindered in business outside their home state, that a few of them called the first Constitutional Convention.

197

"Whatever else goes into the new Constitution," they agreed, "the states must yield to Congress the right to regulate commerce across state lines. If business is to grow, it needs uniform laws."

Which applied to the present case, the Fifth Amendment or the Interstate Commerce cause? It was not a matter of law, but of viewpoint.

"There is no connection between interstate commerce and labor unions," decided a majority of the Supreme Court. "The Act is unconstitutional."

Once again Oliver Wendell Holmes appealed to his fellow judges not to deny the will of the people. "Let us save the Act as long as there is a way to do so. Here is the way: Strikes and labor trouble on railroads affect interstate commerce. The people's representatives think that by building a strong labor union, it will prevent strikes. What we judges think of the wisdom of the plan is irrelevant. The law of the land must help the people in their collective needs."

To help the people in their needs! Judge Holmes always looked at the law with this ideal in his mind. And whenever he felt that his fellow judges were unsympathetic with those needs, he did not keep quiet, but wrote down one of his many famous dissenting opinions.

Never was he more disappointed with the Supreme Court's failure to help the people than in

1917. The year before, Congress had considered the evil of child labor. Some states had already rid themselves of the evil. But in others, the sight of children of ten entering a mine or factory at the break of day was common. Everyone admitted the shame of it, but child labor was profitable to employers. What could Congress do?

It could not enter a state and forbid child labor. Such is the peculiar history of the nation that the Constitution does not give Congress that right. Once the states were separate colonies of England. When England was driven out, each colony was left sovereign unto itself. Need forced the sovereign states to unite under a constitution. But jealously, under the Tenth Amendment, they reserved to themselves all the rights not delegated to the United States. No, Congress could not say to a factory owner: "You may not employ children under fourteen." The factory owner could reply: "Only my State Legislature has the right to say so." But one thing Congress could do, it thought; it could forbid the interstate shipment of goods from factories employing children under fourteen. That would stop child labor. And such a law Congress passed.

At once a cry arose from the cotton-mill owners of the South. However worded, they protested, the law really said: "You may not employ children under fourteen." In the sacred names of Liberty and the Constitution they carried their protest to the bench of the Supreme Court.

And they won. When the Chief Justice counted the votes, there were five on one side and four on the other. With a majority of one, the Supreme Court struck out the law against child labor, and corporations regained the liberty to ruin the lives of children in factory or mine.

But the voice of Judge Holmes again rang out in dissent. States Rights, true. Liberty, of course. These words, what do they mean? They meant one thing one hundred and fifty years ago, and another thing to-day. The word "road" then meant a wagon path through an otherwise unbroken wilderness; "light" meant a candle; "travel," a rare experience in a stagecoach. He himself had lived before the time of bathtubs and sewing machines, when Texas was not in the United States, when farmers harvested their grain with scythe and sickle. Life changes and grows, and with it the lexicon of life. The ideas of the nineteenth century will not do for the twentieth. The ideas of the Constitution must expand with the country; otherwise the nation will burst through it as through a choking garment. Liberty? Whose liberty? That is the question. We live in a society. At every step the individual's liberty is curtailed for the sake of the citizen's.

"If there is any matter upon which civilized

countries have agreed," he said, "it is the evil of premature and excessive child labor." The law seemed to Judge Holmes constitutional. For the cry "Our liberty is in danger," when it really meant "Our profits are in danger," Judge Holmes had no ear. But he who once had offered his life in the cause of freedom knew of what it consisted, and where the Constitution proclaimed it.

In 1917, when American troops were sent into Russia after the Revolution there, a group of Russian-born people printed two leaflets which they circulated. Both leaflets called the President uncomplimentary names because he sent troops into Russia, and they exhorted the workers of America to stand by the workers of Russia.

"Awake! Awake! You workers of the world!" they shrieked in tall words, and were signed "Revolutionists."

When these revolutionary leaflets fell into the hands of agents of the Department of Justice, four men and a girl were arrested and sentenced to twenty years' imprisonment. They appealed until finally they stood before the Supreme Court of the land.

"I believe," said Judge Holmes, "that the defendants had as much right to publish these leaflets as the Government has to publish the Constitution of the United States." Were the defendants being punished for their beliefs? he asked. "Time has upset many fighting faiths. . . . The best test of truth is the power of the thought to get itself accepted in the competition of the market. . . . That is the theory of our Constitution. It is an experiment as all life is an experiment.

"Congress shall make no law . . . abridging the freedom of speech," he quoted.

But again he spoke in dissent, addressing the future.

For fifty years Judge Holmes served on the bench. On his ninetieth birthday, the most prominent jurists of the country joined in celebrating the event. Their praises and gratitude and love for him circulated widely in books and journals. They called him the greatest living jurist of the English-speaking world, one of the greatest of all time. They recalled the startling brilliance of this or that opinion of his. They exchanged stories of his wit, or of his charity. He was not only a jurist; he was a sage and a poet whose thought brushed the stars.

Professionally, lawyers and judges were in his debt. They used his work on Common Law and other legal branches constantly. But more importantly, he had given them a purpose and a faith. Law, Holmes taught them, was a battleground in the struggle between past rights and present needs. In the struggle, the duty of the lawyer or judge

202

was to help the present as it changed into the future.

"Provide for change," warned Judge Holmes, "for it is coming."

He had set them precedents. His opinions on the new problems of the community, such as labor and child welfare, blazed for them the legal way onward. He had shown how to treat words like "liberty" or "equality" or "property," so as not to thwart the will of the living generation.

"The Constitution is not the scolding voice of the past," he seemed to say, "nor is it an old strait jacket. It is a flexible instrument, meant by our forefathers to be helpful if managed properly."

Where the past and present faced each other, he always judged the present to have the right of way, so that it might come peacefully into the future. Any other judgment to him was undemocratic.

"Much that we hold dear must be done away with, short of revolution, by orderly change of law," he said.

He was not afraid of change. He taught sympathy with the living, not worship of the dead. "Invincibly young," he was called at ninety, and the bold and brilliant young minds of the nation looked to him as one of their leaders.

His youth consisted not in lack of years, but in holding close in his spirit the spirit of America. Let

us not be afraid, he says to his fellow American.
We will take our chances on the hard road of Democracy. Above all, we will be tolerant of our
fellow-travelers, whoever they are, for we all have
the same Bill of Rights.

"The deepest cause we have to love our country," he said gallantly, "is that instinct, that spark,
that makes the American unable to meet his fellow man otherwise than simply as a man, eye to
eye, hand to hand, and foot to foot, wrestling
naked on the sand."

9
The Grand Old Man of Labor

SAMUEL GOMPERS

Where everyone is free to express his will, life has a strenuous and a hopeful beauty. Usually, however, no citizen stands alone in his need. There are many like him. Sometimes a leader rises among like-minded people. He reminds them that in union there is strength, and then unites their wills into one Group Will. Democracy is largely a check and balance of groups.

SAMUEL GOMPERS *was such a group leader.*

THE GRAND OLD MAN OF LABOR

I

HE heard the cry first in the street where he lived on the East end of London, and for the rest of his life the cry kept ringing in his ears. He was a small boy then with his nose flat against the windowpane. The tramping on the cobbles outside drew him often to the window, and he watched men, the fathers and older brothers of his playmates, moving aimlessly about. They gathered in groups; they drifted apart and together again, like scraps of rubbish blown about in the back yard. And the cry of one of them penetrated the shut window and lodged in his brain: —

"God, I've no work to do. My wife, my kids want bread, and I've no work to do."

When Sam was a grown-up of ten, his father took him out of the free school for Jewish boys, and apprenticed him to a shoemaker. His father himself was by trade a cigarmaker. Often after

supper he rose from the table saying he was off
to a meeting of the Cigarmakers' Society.

"I would rather be a cigarmaker," remarked
Sam, the shoemaker of eight weeks standing.

"And why?" asked father Gompers.

"Because shoemakers have no society," replied
Sam.

With that, the Society of Cigarmakers enrolled
a new apprentice boy. Sam took his place at a long
worktable. In the daily company of men his raw,
open mind was molded as tightly as the rich brown
velvety leaves of tobacco molded between his
fingers. They talked of hard times, of wages and
starvation in England. Some spoke of a land to the
west, where wages were higher and they sang: —

To the West, to the West, to the land of the free
Where mighty Missouri rolls down to the sea;
Where a man is a man if he's willing to toil,
And the humblest may gather the fruits of the soil.

Yet even there a civil war had broken out over the
freedom of workers. The English factory owners,
Sam heard, were on the side of the South; but the
working class was with Lincoln. In the whole world,
Abraham Lincoln had no more loyal admirer than
the thirteen-year-old boy Sam Gompers. When
his father, one day, announced gloomily that to
save themselves from starvation they would have

to leave England for America, Sam thrillingly thought that he would be closer to Abraham Lincoln. His father, who once before had been driven to break the ties of family and friends by emigrating from Amsterdam to London, was in despair.

Between the East end of London and the East Side of New York there was only a step: the struggle to pay the landlord and the grocer was unchanged. The one difference for Sam lay in the many and different races of people he accosted this side of Castle Garden. His new fellow countrymen greeted him in a score of tongues. The shop where he found work was manned mostly by Germans. But at the Cooper Institute where he attended lectures and night school, his American friends were also Irish, Bohemian, Russian, Swedish.

Most of his education came to him with his wages; the shop was his university. He grew to manhood in an atmosphere choked and blended with tobacco dust. All day long he took the soft leaves stripped off their stems, one by one off the pile. He examined the leaf, and shaved off the frayed edge to a hair's breadth. Then he wrapped it around the sausage of tobacco, deftly knitting the holes in the leaf and shaping the cigar.

He enjoyed the work because, once his fingers had become expert, his mind was left free. Cigar-makers could cultivate one another's society during working hours.

"Sing us something, Otto," they coaxed. And high above the littered bench rose the dreamy spirit of the song

Kennst du das land . . .

Sometimes it was, "Read to us, Sam." Sam had a strong, mellow voice and there was always a book or magazine in his pocket. Discussion always followed reading. Always they argued some question or other, rarely deciding anything but heaps of cigars. Now and then Sam would hastily draw out a pencil and piece of paper, and note down a striking thought or hint for homework.

"But Karl Marx says . . ." someone would remark — and Sam made the note that he must learn German, must read Karl Marx.

They talked of themselves, of their lot as workers and citizens — Sam now a voter. At such times a mood of despair prevailed, because the days of the cigarmakers seemed numbered. From every quarter they discerned threats to their existence. A tool had been invented for molding cigars, and the craftsmen saw in it a portent of the time when their skill would be thrown into the discard.

"Either we destroy the machine, or it will destroy us," believed some of Samuel Gomper's shopmates.

"But to destroy the machine is to stop the wheels of progress," objected Sam.

Then the "sweatshop" menaced them. Some merchants had bought up a block of tenements. There they installed families of immigrants whom they put to work making cigars. The immigrant family paid rent to the merchant, was forced to buy their raw tobacco and tools from him, their food even. The cigar merchant paid little for his labor, had no rent to pay for a factory, and made profit on the sale of provisions. Naturally he was able to sell his cigars at astoundingly low prices. But at whose expense? Samuel Gompers visited "sweatshops." He found that merely to keep alive, every member of the "sweatshop" family had to work early and late, seven days a week. The low price of the "sweatshop" cigar dragged down the price of the factory cigar, and that in turn beat down the wages of all craftsmen like Samuel Gompers. They found themselves unable any longer to provide their families with decent food or living quarters. The cigar smoker was content, the cigar manufacturer also, but the worker was desperate.

"Sweatshops are degrading," Sam and his friends agreed bitterly.

Then in 1873 another depression paralyzed the industry of the country. Through the blizzards of the winter Samuel Gompers saw the lines of men outside the free-soup kitchens in every ward. What knew those bewildered, suffering men of stock-market deflation or bank credits? They knew only that they begged for work and were turned away, that their families were hungry.

Again the cry rang in the ears of Samuel Gompers: —

"God, I've no work to do. My wife, my kids want bread, and I've no work to do."

Was there no answer to this cry? Some of his friends had panaceas for poverty.

"The Government should print paper money," they said. "Then money will be so plentiful that we can all have some."

"Reduce the hours of work," others said. They put their idea into the slogan: "Eight hours for work. Eight hours for rest. Eight hours for what we will."

"If the Government owned all industries," contended others, "the workers would be well off."

Samuel Gompers shook his head. He knew of no cure-all for the ills of the workingman. He knew only his distress. And he pitied him and stood ready to risk his own welfare to help him.

Sam Gompers' shopmates often told what he once risked for "Conchy."

"Conchy," as he was nicknamed, was a middle-aged sick man with very weak eyes. Sam Gompers and he worked at a bench near the windows of the dim factory. One morning when Sam came to work, he found Conchy sitting at a bench in the dimmest part of the factory.

Sam went to him. "What's the matter?" he asked.

"They put me back here and gave that new young fellow my seat near the window," Conchy said plaintively.

"What for?"

"Well, they just put him there, that's all. I don't know why."

Sam went back to his seat and sent a callboy to Mr. Smith, the new foreman. The boy came back with word that Mr. Smith was busy.

"Tell him please it's important," insisted Sam.

Mr. Smith arrived. "Well, what do you want?" he demanded.

"Why did you put Conchy away back in the dark and the young fellow down here in the light?" asked Sam.

With an oath the foreman rapped: "None of your business."

Conchy was an old employee, Sam pointed out; his sight had failed in the work. The young fellow —

"That's my business," said the foreman.

"You mean to say you're going to let the young fellow keep Conchy's seat?"

"Yes, I am. What are you going to do about it?"

Sam rose. He gathered up his tools. "Not much," he said, "except that he can have this seat, too."

There was a second of silence. Then a voice broke out — "Yes, and he can have this seat, too."

Another man rose: "And this seat."

Fifty men pushed back their chairs: "And this seat."

The men had struck.

Five minutes later the strike was settled. The factory was working as usual, with Conchy back in his old seat.

"If we always acted together," Sam Gompers told his shopmates, "we should never be either standing in free-soup lines, or working twelve hours every day."

That was his answer to the cry in the streets, the cry he could never forget since his childhood in London when he preferred the trade of cigar-making to shoemaking because cigarmakers had a "Society."

"Let us act together," was not a new appeal in America, even among workingmen. For almost fifty years before Samuel Gompers came to work in America, workers had sometimes united to parade their grievances. In such unions the shoe-makers and printers protested against low wages, the hatters and other factory hands against their fourteen hours of daily toil. The bricklayers, the plasterers, the plumbers — good men of toil — organized societies. Intelligent workers realized that if ever they were to rise out of the cellars in

214

the slums where so many of them lived, they would have to stand united. But these unions were temporary. When indignation welled up in a trade, the workers rushed together; when their indignation was appeased or routed, they drifted apart.

"What labor needs," said Sam and his friends, speaking of the sweatshops and soup kitchens, "what labor needs is permanent strong unions."

The cigarmakers' local union, to which Sam had belonged since the age of fourteen, was a crude club and yet as good as any of that time. It maintained little order or discipline among its members. Any day in any shop, a worker might suddenly throw down his tools and remark angrily: "I am going on strike." If enough of his friends followed him, perhaps there was a strike. But few strikes begun like that ended successfully for the workers. There was even, in New York City, a council of all crafts, called the Workingmen's Association. Perhaps its most notable act was to give Samuel Gompers the opportunity of making his first public speech. It happened in a mass meeting that the twenty-four-old cigarmaker rose to stammer out his feeling against sweatshops. When he sat down, one of the labor officials — a German — said kindly to him: "That was all right, Sam. You will yet a good speaker be."

Sam had made a start. As he saw it, industry was a jungle infested by beasts of prey in the shape

215

of low wages and long hours, and withstanding them timidly the patchwork of labor groups. To civilize the jungle, the labor patchwork would have to be knit together more solidly. Only then could the worker win a seat alongside his employer, and together lay down plans for their common welfare.

"That's a good talk, Sam," said his friends over their mugs of beer. "Now what would you do to strengthen the Cigarmaker's Union?"

To begin with, thought Sam, there were too many small unions of cigarmakers. They must give way to one big union. Its constitution would resemble the charter of an American city divided into wards over which sat a council. The shops were wards which elected delegates to the Union Council. And in all disputes with employers over the conditions of work, the Council would govern. . . .

"That's the kind of union I should like to see," said Sam.

So began Cigarmakers' Local Number 144. Its president, Samuel Gompers, remarked that it was democratic in form, and strongly knit because every member, no matter where he worked, committed himself to help every other member in debates with his employer over wages and working conditions. To their delight, the cigar workers early began to reap the benefits of their union in Local Number 144, and the name Samuel Gompers became popular among the working class throughout New York City.

But not among certain employers. For if the workers' lot was improved, their employers' profits were cut down. Some employers resented this. In their own councils they hissed the name of Samuel Gompers. Once his boss summoned Sam to the office. Both men, face to face, respected each other; Sam for his boss's kindness, and the boss for Sam's fine work at the bench.

"Sam," said his boss in a distressed voice, "I needn't tell you what I think of you and your work. But the employers' organization to which I belong has voted to blacklist the leaders of the recent strike."

"Which means" — Sam helped him say it — "that I'm out of a job. It's not your fault."

When he got back to the shop to pack his tools, his fellow workers indignantly rose to declare a strike. Sam climbed on a chair — he now made speeches without stammering — and the men gathered around him. . . . It was contrary to the rules of Local Number 144 to walk out in that fashion. They must be loyal not to him, but to the whole union; they must stay at work. . . . And they did.

He found a job with a manufacturer who did not belong to an employers' association. One day his new boss summoned him to his office.

217

"Won't you sit down, Mr. Gompers. Mr. Gompers, how would you like to be my foreman at twenty-five dollars a week?"

Sam was then earning twelve dollars. He waited to hear more.

"In fact, I look to you," said his boss, "to become my superintendent. And that is not all. If you will induce the union workers to take a reduction in pay, you can have half what I save. With your influence, it ought to be easy."

So that was it. Sam did not waste more time before packing his tools than was necessary to repay the insult. His haste swept him out before he could raise a nickel for carfare, and he walked home. He did not mind that, nor the winter slush, nor his torn shoes. If he was beside himself with anguish, the reason was his wife and kids. They would dine again on a soup of flour and water. One employer, realizing his staunchness, had sent a messenger to his wife offering her thirty dollars a week if she could induce Sam to give up the union. His loyal wife had refused. But was he fair to her and the children? He might give in, and ease the suffering of his family. But he thought of all the workers and their families, and their faith in him.

He talked the matter over with a few other leaders in the labor unions. "Let us pledge each other," he proposed, "never to rise outside the labor movement." And together they swore, like

218

monks taking holy vows. Their purpose was to show the workers of every trade why and how they should combine in unions, so that no employer could refuse to deal with them as equals. In his vision, Sam Gompers saw the time when employer and worker — labor and capital — would sit at the same table, and talk frankly and freely of each other's needs and problems. Then, he felt, there would be no more misery among the toiling citizens of America. The vision was inspiring, but it could never become real, Sam knew, until labor stood so united that reluctant capital would not dare refuse its coöperation.

As he had been one of the principal organizers of the Cigarmakers' Local Number 144, Sam helped also to organize a union of all the trades in New York City, called the Amalgamated Trades and Labor Union. He believed that not only must one cigarmaker stand with another, one printer with another, every man with the men of his trade, but every worker must stand by every other worker. A certain Government official understood Sam Gompers, for he said: "Mr. Gompers" — the labor leader had apologized for coming to him on this occasion — "Mr. Gompers, I regard you as the spokesman for the underdog of the world."

Now, with the force of organized labor behind him, Samuel Gompers attacked the cigar sweatshops. He set about educating the public, educating representatives of the people elected to the Legislature. He showed, publicly and privately, pictures of rooms in tenement houses where children as young as six, pale and weary, squatted on a dirty floor, stripping tobacco until late in the night or until they fell over with fatigue on the tobacco heap.

The sweatshop merchants retaliated. They denied those pictures, and produced more favorable ones. They fought by advertisement, they went to law. The battle against the cigar sweatshops lasted more than ten years, but victory came finally to the forces of organized labor.

Samuel Gompers was learning how to make social change in a democracy. Though young, he knew already how to organize for the protection of workers. He was satisfied with labor unions in his own city. Now he turned his attention to the labor union of the whole country.

He talked about it with men of various trades. Many an evening, after the day's work, he sat down at a table in some public place to discuss his pet hope — the Federation of American Labor. His boon companions were printers, carpenters, tailors, stonecutters — any workers who belonged to the union of their trade. Employers were wise, Sam felt; throughout the nation they were banding together. In a few trades, the employees were doing the same thing. All the local unions of cigar-makers, for instance, had affiliated as the International Cigarmakers; likewise the printers. On special occasions a national union held a convention where a few delegates met, passed some resolutions, and went home. That was fine, agreed Sam; he would like to see those national unions stronger. But they treated of matters in their own trade. They were like State Legislatures. Now just as all the states were federated, as the United States of America, all trade-unions of the country ought likewise to federate. Such was his plan for the welfare of the American worker.

But, some people objected, the American worker already had a national union of all trades: the Knights of Labor. In December of 1869, nine tailors of Philadelphia had started the Knights of Labor, a union of workers of every kind in the country. Their purpose was to improve the lot of the American worker. The Knights of Labor were growing. Was not that the answer to Sam Gompers' hope?

No, said Sam. The purpose of the Knights of Labor was good, but they would never achieve it by their method. Take, for instance . . .

By two o'clock in the morning, Sam usually convinced or wore out his opponents.

For almost ten years Samuel Gompers preached

his favorite sermon: the Federation of American
Labor. As the father of a big family, he could ill
afford to travel, yet he went out to distant conventions of labor unions to deliver his sermon.
Whenever he felt discouraged, he thought of his
fellow workers living in slums, of pale and weary
children in factories, of mayhem and death coming to factory hands with no compensation to their
stricken families. There was his inspiration, and
he came to be known as the spokesman for the
workers of America.

At last, in December of 1886, came the moment
Sam Gompers had worked for. In Columbus, Ohio,
the American Federation of Labor, the union of
all labor unions, was organized. In its constitution
it was modeled after the United States of America.
But just as the States in 1787 did not yield much
power to the Federal Government, so the labor
unions did not yield much power to their Federation. Weak as it was, however, it was the realiza-
tion of Sam Gompers' dream. If its president were
skillful and devoted, it would grow.

No one wanted the presidency of the new American Federation of Labor, for the office paid a
salary of only one thousand dollars a year. One
could hardly support a family on that. Samuel
Gompers, father of the Federation, was first nominated. He declined. But when the subsequent
nominees also declined, he stepped forward for

another sacrifice in behalf of the working class of his country.

Shortly after, John Doe read "in the papers" of the American Federation of Labor, and saw the picture of its president: a short, stocky individual, with black hair and dark snapping eyes. It was a picture John Doe was to see often in the years to come.

II

His first office in New York, at 332 East Eighth Street, was no more commodious than a pantry. It had a kitchen table for a desk. The rest of the office equipment consisted of empty grocer's boxes. Thus installed, Samuel Gompers began his new life as professional agent of labor. Heretofore he had been concerned largely with the problems only of his own trade, cigarmaking. Now his concern was with the problems of every trade. He learned to speak of his work with the glassblower and the steamfitter, as with the tailor and carpenter. They, in turn, listened more readily to his appeal to stand united in their trade, to add their trade-union to all others in the Federation. From all parts of the country workers came to him and wrote to him for advice and help.

Thus he became aware of the griefs and griev-

223

ances of all workers, and he spoke for them. . . .
Are the men in the steel mills of Western Pennsylvania required to work twelve hours a day? One
morning the president of the steel company re-
ceives a courteous letter from Samuel Gompers,
who suggests a friendly talk about the welfare of
his employees. . . . The garment workers are
protesting the unsafe and unsanitary condition of
factories: and the factory owners have to reckon
with Samuel Gompers. . . . Out on the West
Coast the seamen are realizing that, in a democratic world, they alone are bound like serfs to the
sea by the rule that they must not quit their ship
even in a safe harbor. One day they come upon
notices of a seamen's meeting called by Samuel
Gompers. Mr. Gompers encourages them to stand
united in their fight. Congressmen have a visit
from Mr. Gompers, who explains the slavery of
seamen, and suggests a new law. Congressmen get
used to seeing Mr. Gompers. He comes on various
errands. Now he represents a body of voters who
protest the cruelty of child labor; now he appears
in Congress to plead for the unemployed who have
wives and kids to feed, and no work to do. We
have a rich land, says Mr. Gompers warmly. Yet
we allow our abundant tools to rust and our fertile
soil to lie fallow while people starve. It is stupid
and brutal.

Wherever he appeared and on whatever occasion, Samuel Gompers contended that the American worker had the right to a better life.

Nor was the struggle for the worker's rights always to be fought in a swivel chair. Sometimes it took a sinister form, and at such times Samuel Gompers sallied into the field like a crusader in a holy cause.

One pictures him, for instance, as the coal miners of Pennsylvania and West Virginia saw him in the '90's. Out of curiosity or hopelessness, groups of miners gathered at the roadside or in a hall to hear the stranger from New York. He told them first what they themselves knew too sorrowfully, but they marveled that any outsider should know or care: They lived lives of bondage; their homes were shacks owned by the coal company. The food they ate and the clothes they wore had to be bought from the coal company. Their sons were brought into the world by the company's doctor; at the age of eight sent into the company's mines; clothed and fed from the company's stores, buried in the company's graveyard. They were slaves. . . . And what did he advise? They must unite and demand, like self-respecting men, a decent life.

The coal companies resented Samuel Gompers; he was attacking their profits, and they tried to drive him from their towns. Their lawyers arraigned him in court. The labor leader hurt their business, they maintained; his talk was illegal.

Speech is free in America, replied Samuel Gompers.

But he was inciting the men to strike, said the protectors of profit. Strikes hurt the country; therefore he, Samuel Gompers, was his country's enemy. . . .

Samuel Gompers was not frightened by such attacks. He felt that his thinking compatriots would see through them. But too frequently strikes did break out, sometimes with violent accompaniment of mob scenes, fights, and bloodshed. At such times, the public was shocked, and demanded that workers and their employers settle their disputes peaceably.

Strikes distressed Samuel Gompers more than anyone else, and he tried all fair means to avoid them. He knew the suffering a strike brought down on the very workers he wished to help. But sometimes he was powerless to prevent a strike. At other times, however, when every other means had failed to abolish the wrongs to a group of workers, he shouldered the responsibility and fearlessly called for a strike.

In a republic, he said, strikes were necessary. They were like pain in the social body. They forced people's attention to a disease, and resulted in better industrial health. Employers and workers understood each other better after they had suf-

226

fered in a strike, and the nation thereby gained. "I trust that the day will never come when the workers surrender their right to strike," he said.

He upheld the workers' right to strike because he believed in democracy. To him democracy was like a strenuous game in which groups of people joined together as in teams, for their common advantage. The zest and beauty of the game was that each player was free to choose his side. Employers lined on one side of the field, for example; workers on the opposite. Of course this sort of play was not for children. The contestants were in deadly earnest, hurt and scarred in the brunt of battle. But if the rules of the game were observed, it developed the players as did no other form of political life. . . . But the rules must be observed. To those who would prevent him from advising the workers of the country he warned: Mind the rules of democracy — free speech. Those employers who would prevent their workers from forming unions he warned: You are violating a rule of freedom. Employers unite; workers have the right to do likewise.

The employers of the country must learn, moreover, that the way to avoid strikes of their workers is not by opposing their unions, but by collaborating with them and sharing their problems. The good of the country demands a common council of labor and capital.

For forty years Samuel Gompers stood as on a platform, gavel in hand, his dark eyes snapping and his voice raised to implant his ideas for the worker's welfare in the conscience of his country. Led by him, the trade-unions flourished. He himself came to be regarded as one of the leaders of America. To many his life was like a fairy tale. "Once there was a little cigarmaker" — so the story might begin — "and he looked about him and saw Evil Things crushing the Man in Overalls. So the little cigarmaker fashioned a weapon called Trade-Unionism, and went forth to do battle with the Labor Evils in the shape of Long Hours and Low Wages. . . ." The romance told of young Samuel Gompers in his office furnished with empty grocers' boxes. That was long ago, in the days when he was little known. But in the ripeness of time, he became a mighty champion, and a power in the land to be feared and loved. Then his office contained desks and secretaries in the elegant American Federation of Labor building, within walking distance of the White House. The dwellers in the White House often called for the advice of Mr. Gompers. The little cigarmaker was not abashed, not even when he was guest to the King of Great Britain, whose ragged subject he once was. He was not abashed because he, too, represented a mighty power, Labor. He had taught Labor the value of acting through union. He had shown Capital the necessity of deliberating with Labor on their common welfare.

The real romance in the life of Samuel Gompers was his devotion to what he called "the holy cause of labor." Worldly men who appreciated his talents offered him on several occasions fortunes in money if he would give up his holy cause and enter business. But he preferred to live in his small house, comparatively poor, and continue his devotions in the holy cause. Once a capitalist proposed to him that he become the president of a corporation about to operate in Mexico. The corporation intended to run farms on a gigantic scale. With the cheap labor there, said the capitalist, millions in profits were to be made in Mexico. Now, Samuel Gompers had been thinking of Mexico. He himself was about to operate there, because of cheap labor. He intended, in fact, to make it less cheap. He declined the business offer, of course; he had other profits in mind, holier ones. His business in Mexico was to uplift the degraded worker, the peon, until he stood shoulder to shoulder with his neighbor, the worker across the Rio Grande.

In the fall of 1924, the American Federation of Labor was holding its annual convention at El Paso. Its founder, "the Grand Old Man of Labor," still sat in the presidential chair. This was fated to be the last time he would face his flock. But he did not know that. In Juarez across the Rio Grande, another mighty organization of workers, the Mexican Federation of Labor, had also convened, and to the lips of their speakers one word, a name, came often. It fell on the air with the hush of a sacred word, and then the air blazed with a *"Viva!"* The word was Gompers. The Grand Old Man did not know that. But one day one thousand men marched across the International Bridge and into the hall where he sat, gavel in hand. He had dreamed of this moment, when the foreign workers would sit in common council with the American. His other dream, of workers sharing in the councils of their employers and of the Government — that had already come true. Now this. His mission in life, he felt, was fulfilled; he was ready to die, and no regret.

Catching sight of the old man on the platform, the Mexicans, some of them barefooted, burst into wild applause. They cheered him, they sang to him; a few of them fell on their knees before him, blessing him for what he had done to free them from peonage.

The program of the convention called for the election of a president. Now, except for one year, Samuel Gompers had been re-elected every year for forty years. Times had changed, however. Many delegates disagreed with the old man's policies. They felt that younger labor leaders, new ideas, should prevail.

The old man looked worn out. His days were numbered. . . . A delegate rose and nominated Samuel Gompers for president, and the motion was seconded. Not a delegate present but felt that whatever his disagreement with the old man, he owed him every homage in his final hours. For the cause of labor alone, the Grand Old Man had consecrated his life. More than any other man in the country, it was he who had given Labor a voice. And that voice he had trained until it was heard with respect throughout the world, for it spoke in the interests of the workers. . . .

So Samuel Gompers was elected unanimously. The Grand Old Man was chief to the last.

10

Up from Slavery

BOOKER T. WASHINGTON

About the time that Samuel Gompers began his service to democracy, BOOKER TALIAFERRO WASHINGTON *began his. The men and their methods were unlike each other. In one sense, however, they were alike: they both struggled for the uplift of a group.*

UP FROM SLAVERY

He had stood before kings. The president of his country had consulted him on matters of state. Every day, in his huge bundle of mail, he found the usual invitations: "Our town would be honored by your presence." He was a powerful man and in the prime of life, but for all his duties he needed the strength of three men. People referred to him as one of the leaders of his country. It was quite natural, therefore, that he should be asked to tell the story of his life.

He was still too busy with the future to turn his thoughts to the past, but he felt that the story of his struggles might bring to his despairing people a message of hope. So, on the run, at railroad stations and on board trains, in hotels and at home during odd moments — he cast the line of his thoughts into the dark stream of the past.

"I was born a slave on a plantation," he began. He did not know exactly the place or date, but it was somewhere in Franklin County, Virginia, in

235

1858 or 1859. "Of my ancestry I know almost nothing." His mother was the plantation cook and with her he lived in a small cabin that had no windows, no floor but the naked earth.

Snatches of his childhood rose up. He saw himself again an urchin scarcely more than just born, cleaning the yards, taking water to the men in the fields and corn to the mill. Once he saw some of the white folk eating ginger-cakes, and was inspired with his first ambition. Some day, he vowed, when he got big he too would eat ginger-cakes. That is, providing he were free. Just then, he wasn't. He knew, because once in the darkness he awoke to see his mother on her knees over him, and his brother and sister praying God for Lincoln and his army.

One night there was more than the usual singing in the slave quarter. The songs were louder, more joyous.

> A band of angels comin' after me
> Comin' for to carry me home.

And early the next morning his mother took him and his brother and sister to the "big house," which was the master's. All the slaves had gathered around the porch, listening to a strange man in uniform who made a speech and read a long paper to them. He could not understand the man, but his mother bent trembling over him and wet his face with her tears and kisses.

"We are free," she whispered.

Free! To the ragged and homeless black folk what did the word mean? Did it mean that now they could talk with their friends when they willed, would dance and sing, could wander over the face of the land, free to own each his plot of ground and raise hogs and chickens and crops? At any rate, the urchin found himself jogging beside a cart with his mother over the mountains until they came at last to a cluster of huts called Malden, in the Kanawha Valley, West Virginia. To him Freedom meant from now on getting up at four in the morning to work in the salt furnace outside the town.

In the salt furnace a new ambition awoke in him. His barrels were marked by the foreman with mysterious figures. He learned that the figures were the number, 18. He heard of other figures, of print in newspapers and books that some people could decipher. Suddenly he was seized with desire to be like those people. Freedom meant knowledge, and his desire for knowledge buoyed him with ecstasy. He was well-named "Booker."

He shared the ecstasy for learning with his kind, with all the four million restless freedmen. Not one in twenty among them, perhaps, could read and write. In the days of their enslavement their

237

masters, realizing that knowledge meant freedom, had deprived them by law of teachers and schools. But now, felt the ex-slaves, as necessary as having a piece of land was having a school. A spiritual thirst seized the race. The old could not die without reading the Bible; the young could not live without learning.

Sympathetic, the Government built schools for them throughout the South. Their old friends up North sent them schoolmarms. As fast as schools were opened, they were thronged with scholars ranging in age up to seventy-five years, peering into spellers.

With the boy Booker, as with all his race, his desire for education ran ahead of his facilities. There was at first no school in his town. His mother got him a speller, but its mysteries did not detain him long. A young Negro who could read drifted into town, and with him the boy sat up nights. But to Booker this mentor proved no profounder than the speller. At last a school opened just outside the town. The boy heard the news with a thrill, only to find that his family, in their desperate straits, could not spare him from the salt-furnace. With misty eyes he watched other children prance down the road, bound for the temple of learning. The boy kept on praying for his chance, too; and finally, by putting in his time at the furnace before dawn and after dark, he managed to free

238

himself for a few hours during the day. Off he dashed to the schoolhouse. There was no happier boy before the teacher.

At that point Booker was smitten with shame. Every pupil was responding to the roll-call with two names. Some were even the proud announcers of three names. Booker, with only one, thought fast.

"Name?"

It was his turn. "Booker — Washington," he returned calmly. He congratulated himself on his taste in names. Later, when he discovered that at his birth his mother had called him Booker Talia-ferro, he was even more delighted. He too had three names; he was Booker Taliaferro Washing-ton. So History enrolled him.

No sooner had he begun his career as a scholar in the one-room school shack than he was forced to give it up for work in a coal mine. Pick in hand, the twelve-year-old boy lived his day underground by the light flickering from his cap. He learned well and bitterly the lesson on the advantages to life of the sun and wind. Groping about once he learned what to him was more than the doubtful advantage of life. Cavernous echoes brought to him the talk of two fellow miners. They were talk-ing of a school for colored people, somewhere in Virginia. The boy crept closer; around him the hollow earth spoke oracularly. He heard how in

239

that school students might work their way through, and learn a trade. . . . When the boy climbed out of the tunnel into the light of day, he had risen from the dead of no hope.

A year and a half later, he bade farewell to his mother. She was spent with disease, and mother and son felt they were parting forever. But the air was gay, for the older folks had come to see him off on his adventure. A short time ago they had all been slaves, and now here was one of their boys off to boarding school. Just like white folks. Presents there were, coins and handkerchiefs, and sound advice.

He was bound for the Hampton Institute, five hundred miles away. On the road over the mountains, his stagecoach stopped at an inn one night. The boy followed the other passengers inside and when everyone else had been shown to a room, stepped shyly up. He had no money, but he would explain that he was on his way to a great school. Before he could, however, the innkeeper had taken one look at him and ordered him out. But, protested the boy, it was night, he felt cold. The innkeeper would not listen. Under the cold starlight, beating his arms across his body, the trembling boy learned the color of his skin.

He had to get to the Hampton Institute somehow. Most of the time he walked. He feasted largely on his hopes, but when he got too hungry he stopped long enough to work for food. Sleeping quarters were easier to find: he lay down on the open ground. But every day brought him nearer the Hampton Institute, nearer the education for which the ex-slave yearned like a fluttering thing for light, for only through education was life endurable.

II

Retracing each step in his past life, Dr. Washington — invited guest of Queen Victoria and President Theodore Roosevelt, and one of America's household names — came to the moment of his greatest decision. His heart had guided him to that decision, which was to give his life to his suffering race of black Americans. That happened when, as a graduate of Hampton Institute, he had returned to his home town, Malden.

He was only seventeen years old then, and chosen to teach a school of colored children. He was prepared to teach his pupils the usual studies bound in books. "Book learning" was what the Negroes wanted as an emblem of their newly got freedom. But when the youthful teacher faced his class, he saw the need of lessons not in books.

He saw his people starting up the ladder of American civilization. Through no fault of their

241

own they were just then at the lowest rung, and their habits matched their position. The young teacher saw before him pupils who wore clothes without care, who had no use for soap, who had never heard of a toothbrush. They had no homes; they took shelter in shacks where the furniture consisted of upturned boxes.

Their former masters had not permitted them to learn the meaning of home. And their former masters seemed determined that the Negro should never learn the meaning of home. By force and by law, the Negro of the South was held at the bottom of the ladder. Rarely was he allowed to vote. Rarely was he shown the decency common to the white American. He could neither walk in the same park nor ride in the same car with the white man. A thousand insults were hurled at him. If he resented the insults, his life was at stake. Enraged at having lost his slaves, the white Southerner declared the Negro unfit to vote or to educate himself, unfit to be a citizen of his country.

"My people are not ready for great book learning," thought Booker Washington. "They must first learn the ways of civilized life: yes, even to the use of soap and the making of a bed. They must win the respect of their white fellow countrymen."

His task seemed impossible. How could he teach the refinements of life — the daily bath — to people who hadn't the daily crust of bread — the necessities of life? How preach the comforts of home — dainty curtains and regular mealtimes — to a mother who worked outside her house to help keep merely the roof over it? How instill respect for law and study in youths unwatched by a mother? How? Only his unflagging pity could find ways for the teacher.

Among his people in Malden, Booker Washington worked not during school hours, but from the time he got up in the morning until bedtime. He taught day and night and Sunday school. He started and managed a library and a debating society. If that left him any free time, he gave free private lessons. His pupils were all the colored inhabitants of Malden that cared to learn, and he urged them all.

A change came over Malden. Mr. Washington's pupils began to dress with more care. They displayed neckties and ribbons and washed faces. Within the schoolroom the floor, the walls, the books were all as tidy as the pupils themselves. Even the outdoor scenery changed. Flowers and whitewash and repairs transformed the shacks into pleasant cottages. And within one or another of these cottages could always, of an evening, be found Booker Washington — helping a backward student, teaching an old man to read his Bible, comforting a sick one.

243

There was grief in Malden when Mr. Washington left. It happened that among his pupils were six boys whom he had inspired to go to the Hampton Institute, his own alma mater. When the boys arrived at Hampton, the principal found them so well grounded in their studies that he wrote to their teacher offering him a post at the Institute. And since it gave Booker Washington the opportunity to be more useful to his race, he accepted the offer.

At Hampton he distinguished himself by the same passion to uplift his race. The principal noted that his new teacher worked day and night among the students. He noted that the students of his night class, men and women who worked daily in mills and laundries, were never willing to part from Mr. Washington when the dismissal bell rang. There was a group of Indians at the school, sent by the Government from their reservations. The principal was doubtful of the result of mixing the two races. He put the Indians in the charge of Mr. Washington and noticed that under his influence they became friendly to the Negroes, and good students.

One day the principal sent for the young teacher and told him that he had received a letter from some prominent people in Tuskegee, Alabama, asking him to recommend someone capable of taking charge of a Normal School for colored people, about to open in Tuskegee.

244

"They ask for a white man," remarked the principal. "I don't know any. Do you think you could fill the position?"

Booker Washington started in astonishment. He was but twenty-three years old. "I am willing to try."

Several days later, the principal read before the assembly of the school a telegram from Tuskegee: —

"Booker T. Washington will suit us. Send him at once."

III

"Up from Slavery" Dr. Washington called the story of his life. It gave him pleasure to recall that once he had been a slave. He was proud of having overcome obstacles and proudest of being the founder of Tuskegee Institute. But as he looked back over a stretch of twenty years, he realized that only by a miracle of faith could he have done it. The odds had been heavily against him. . . .

When the young "principal" arrived in Tuskegee, he found a small town of about two thousand people. He asked for his school and was almost bowled over to hear that the school had neither building, teachers, nor pupils. What did it have? he asked. It had a law; the Alabama Legislature

245

had voted two thousand a year to be spent on teachers of a Normal School for colored people. Booker Washington was the Normal School. Buildings? Pupils? Teachers? He could do as he pleased.

He felt like taking the nearest road back to Hampton. This was some joke; no one expected him to do the impossible. Most of the white people in the South did not believe the Negro fit for education. Education would only spoil him, they argued. The Negro was created a laborer. To try to make anything else of him was a waste of money and effort. The Alabama Legislature did not mind wasting a little money. But it would provide nothing more.

Yet when Booker Washington reflected that but sixteen years before, he and his race had been slaves, he took heart. He knew his own people, that they would justify any trust. They needed only the opportunity. Even this slight opportunity they could not afford to lose. A critical responsibility had been thrust on his conscience. If he took the grudging offer to build up a school, and failed — and who could blame him? — the white people who were hostile would say: "There! As we thought. The Negro can't be educated. In the future let us save our money." If he rejected the offer, the colored might say: "He has denied his own people." Here was his dilemma.

He spent a month traveling over the country roads of Alabama in a cart drawn by a mule, and saw life among the Negroes of the Cotton Belt. He found the Negro family living in a one-room, leaky cabin. In that one room they slept and ate and did everything but wash, for they had no means of bathing. Their diet consisted of two staples, pork and cornbread. They grew no vegetables or grain because they could not spare an inch of soil for anything but cotton. In the morning Booker Washington saw the family, every member but the baby, with a hoe in one hand and a chunk of pork and cornbread in the other, trooping out to the field. Every day but Sunday they spent thus in the service of King Cotton. The baby was laid at the end of a row of cotton, and at intervals of time its mother would stop to suckle it, so that it too might some day enter the ranks of King Cotton.

Even so the family was always in debt. At Christmas when they paid the landlord his share of the crop and what they owed on his loans to them, they had little left to live on until the next harvest.

"They need to learn industry," thought Booker Washington, "and other skills besides farming. Even as farmers they need to know how to escape the serfdom of King Cotton, to grow other crops. They need houses and furniture — property. With

247

property will come respectability, with respectability the esteem of all white people."

They needed the Tuskegee Normal and Industrial Institute, and he would build it.

The story of Tuskegee Institute is famous. It began on July 4, 1881, in an old church and adjoining shanty, with thirty pupils and Mr. Washington. Both buildings were in such bad repair that when it rained a student was assigned an umbrella to hold over the teacher's head. Fortunately they were not long in finding better quarters. It happened that an old plantation near by was put up for sale. The price was five hundred dollars. The principal had none of it, but he borrowed the money on his own responsibility and proceeded to convert the stables and hen-house into class rooms.

The students helped in the work, and gladly. But when he announced that they were to clear some land for planting, they were not glad and said so. What had clearing land to do with education? They wanted book learning.

But, explained their teacher, working with hands was as educational as working with books. He wanted some of them to learn a trade, others to fit themselves to teach the farmers in the plantation districts. Both required the training of the land. . . . With that he seized an axe and strode off to the woods. The students followed.

The story of Tuskegee Institute is a story of aspiration, of a people's struggle up from slavery to power and dignity. With bare hands was Tuskegee built. As more students came, very often in the way the boy Booker had come to Hampton, it became necessary to board them. The principal rented some shacks and in them the students spent the winter, without beds, without blankets, often without being able to sleep for the cold. They did not complain. They knew Booker Washington's devotion to them. And they were happy to suffer for a better future.

So Booker Washington and his school attracted the attention of the neighborhood, white and black. He explained that, once started, his students would build their own buildings, grow their own food, make their own furniture even.

At once, out of sheer admiration for him, people sent the school contributions, not all money. One gave an old horse, another a rusty plow, a third a quilt.

An old woman, covered in rags, one day hobbled in to see him.

"Mr. Washin'ton," she said. "God knows I spent de bes' days of my life in slavery. God knows I's ignorant an' poor; but I knows you is tryin' to make better men an' better women for de colored race. I ain't got no money, but I wants you to take dese six eggs, what I's been savin' up, an' I wants you to put dese six eggs into de eddication of dese boys an' gals."

Applications began to pour in to "Mr. Washington, Dear Sir," and when he reread those letters after a lapse of almost twenty years, he was again blinded.

"I am a poor boy, and I desire to get an education. I will do any work to pay for my lessons."

"Being poor and fatherless, I have had few advantages, and that is why I have applied to you."

"I have read of your school, and would like so well to come there, but I live so far away that I would not be able to pay my fare from New Orleans and then pay my school expenses."

"Please, sir, let me in. I would be one of the happiest boys in the world if you say I could come."

All of the letters bore the same plea, revealed the race with its hands stretched forth to a vision. Booker Washington was ready to sacrifice himself for the helpless youth that pleaded with him as with a savior, but what could he do for so many of them? His school was poor and small. He needed more buildings, more teachers. He must raise more money.

He shut his desk and journeyed north. Before audiences in New York, Boston, and Philadelphia he told the story of Tuskegee. He went boldly to the houses of the rich and told the same story. He spoke of the struggles of his race to improve their lot; of the suffering of a class of American workers; of their energy and his plans for training it.

They had freed the body of the Negro, was the thought he presented. They must now complete the work of emancipation by freeing his mind. To give the Negro schooling was the highest act of patriotism, for either they would raise him up or, like any ignorant class, he would drag the country down.

Wherever Booker Washington went he added friends to his cause. The newspapers reported his speeches with sympathy. Booker T. Washington, they said, was a credit to any race, and the highest type of speaker; his manner sincere and winning . . . With the funds he thus raised, he went back to Tuskegee and put his students to work digging the foundations for new structures, making furniture, laying bricks, plastering walls. They even baked their own bricks, prepared lumber in their own sawmill, and grew their own food. With their own hands the students built their alma mater.

They did not build for themselves. Now that Tuskegee Institute rose firm and spacious on its foundation, and every student was busy in classroom, shop, or field, its young founder set about making it the central power station for Negro welfare. Booker Washington thought not merely of a school, but of headquarters for the Negro American. He thought primarily not of his students, but of his race. For diplomas and pennants and cheers, as for Latin and Greek and French, and for the rest of college pomp, he had no time. His race could not yet afford such luxuries. Tuskegee Institute was to be the guardian of all Negro Americans, devoted to their welfare.

"Every day here," he told his students, "is a day that belongs to the race."

In 1892 he called together a conference of Negro workers. To Tuskegee they came, most of them farmers of the South, carrying their pack of troubles. Before them stood up Booker Washington, and sounded the keynote of the conference.

"Every colored man owes it to himself, and to his children as well, to secure a home just as soon as possible," he said. With property comes power, he explained. The goal of each of them should be to own his house and farm. Until he did, he was more or less a slave to others. From time to time, therefore, all Negro workers ought to meet for the purpose of discussing ways to greater freedom.

His conference became an annual event when every sort of question for the welfare of the race was aired: how to grow more cotton, to build more schools, to pay off a mortgage.

"I want to show Mr. Washington a turnip I

raised," wrote one farmer when asked whether he was attending the next conference. "I want to tell him how much I have saved as a result of these teachings at the annual meetings."

Everyone felt the wisdom of Booker Washington's belief that the problems of the Negro American would be solved by growing bigger turnips and paying off mortgages.

In the same way he called together the Negro women. He wanted them to learn the domestic virtues of a wife and mother: how to can fruit, how to serve dinner, how to rear children; in general, how to make home attractive and efficient. An elementary matter this might be for other classes of Americans, but for those who had recently been slaves and had never a life of their own, it was just the right training for climbing the ladder of civilization.

Booker Washington was teaching not only the students of Tuskegee. He was lifting up every lowly Negro man, woman, and child. From his office in Tuskegee his influence spread throughout the country, especially its Southern states. There Tuskegee graduates went to build more schools for their race, patterned after Tuskegee.

The eyes of America began to turn in admiration to the figure of Booker Washington.

"He is a leader of his race," was how some people worded their respect for him.

"He is one of the leaders of his country," said others. He who worked for the uplift of others belonged to the whole country.

IV

Booker T. Washington, reflecting on the miracle of his rise from slavery, wondered sadly how much he meant to his country. How much good had he done? The institution he had built, now famous the world over, helped to train thousands of Negro Americans every year. That much gratified him. But concerning another side of his work he was not happy.

He had early seen that he must educate the white people of America, at least some of them; he must reform their attitude toward their Negro neighbors. These people sneered at the subject of Negro education. "Education is not meant for the black man," they said. They recalled his days of slavery, forgetting that the shame was their own. They spoke of his faults, neglecting to mention his virtues. They contrasted him, who had just been released from bondage and was handicapped in every way, with the best of their own race who had had no barriers in his way.

To combat this prejudice Booker Washington became spokesman for his race. He spent much

254

of his time addressing audiences in all parts of the country. At first he had sought opportunities to speak, but his fame as an orator spreading, the time came when he was swamped with invitations.

He pitied any man with racial prejudices, he said. Such feelings were degrading. Even if the Negro is as full of faults as the prejudiced people declare, the remedy is to build him more schools, to give him a chance to correct his faults. If that were done, the white people afflicted with prejudice would be the gainers. There would be less crime and less disease in the country, and better citizens. To object to helping the Negro, therefore, is to be unpatriotic.

He spoke thus to his white audiences. His Negro countrymen he assured that prejudice toward them arose not on account of their color, but on account of their lowly condition. He illustrated his point with a story. An old Negro farmer was asked his name.

"I'll tell you," replied the farmer. "In de old days I lived in a little log cabin on rented land, and had to mortgage my crop every year for food. When I didn't have nothin', in dem days, dey used to call me 'Old Jim' Hill. But now I'se out o' debt; I'se de deeds for fifty acres of land; and I lives in a nice house wid four rooms that's painted inside and outside; I'se got some money in de bank; I'se a taxpayer in my community; I'se educated my children. And now dey calls me 'Mr. James' Hill."

Patience, counseled Booker Washington. When the Negro acquires property and education, like Mr. James Hill, all selfish prejudice toward him will disappear.

His audiences grew ever larger. When he came to speak in whatever town, the largest hall failed to hold the crowds. The leading men of the country, the president himself, paid him their respects. If he boarded a train, numbers of fellow passengers approached him for the privilege of shaking his hand. He had become so famous and popular that a lecture bureau offered him fifty thousand dollars to go on tour. He was a poor man, but the offer did not even tempt him.

"My life work is at Tuskegee," he said. He was glad of his popularity only because it helped his race. "If white people are willing to listen to me," he thought, "they will sympathize with my race. And black people may be inspired to devote themselves to the good of their race."

He knew he was popular. Still he was not prepared for the ovation that greeted him when he went to Europe. He had gone, under doctor's orders, for a rest from overwork. But from the moment he boarded the ship, his trip resembled a speaking tour. Aboard ship, a committee of passengers knocked at the door of his stateroom, requesting that he address an assembly of passengers. When he arrived in Paris or London, the American ambassador called with invitations to dinner. Once he had been a slave boy, living in a one-room shanty. Once he had been refused lodgings because of his color. Once he had slept in the streets of Richmond for lack of money to hire a room. Now he was the guest of kings and queens who complimented him on his great work.

The spotlight of fame which played upon him brought to view Tuskegee and its needs; it enabled the Institute to expand its service and send out more and more men and women trained to help their race; it showed the suffering of the Negro American and, in cash and in sympathy, brought forth help. All that gave him the courage to bear up under the strain of his work.

There were times, however, when hostility and prejudice toward the Negro seemed not to abate, and despair laid hold of him and wrung his soul so that he could hardly check the cry on his lips: "It is hopeless. America is without conscience. Its tolerance is a lie."

Then ghosts of his childhood would stir deep in his memory, and he saw again his uncle tied to a tree, stripped naked and a white man whipping him with a cowhide, and the writhing man crying with each thud on his flesh: "Pray, Master! Pray, Master!" To Dr. Washington it seemed as if all his people were still naked and exposed to the blows of prejudice; and in his heart he faltered as he continued to speak, in the name of his race, words without rancor.

But he held steady his vision on a distant goal. For, he thought, in the long run humanity is fair-minded. The highest type of man, white or black, is always fair-minded and generous. And although the road to real democracy is uphill, humanity is making progress. Only a short while ago the Negro American was a slave. Now he has educated himself, bought himself some property, become successful in many lines, made a name for himself in literature and art. No, concluded Booker Taliaferro Washington, despair was uncalled for.

His own rise up from slavery was a story that rang with hope and the promise of a brighter day.

II

The Good Neighbor

JANE ADDAMS

The banners of Liberty and Equality fly at high mast. Yet the nation is afflicted with a daily burden of misery. In every slum, in every congested street, there goes on a pitiless waste of human life. There is no single cause; tears have many causes. That much of the burden can and ought to be lightened — that is the faith of democracy.

JANE ADDAMS took the purpose of democracy to be simply human welfare. Her career began one day when she felt a rush of pity.

THE GOOD NEIGHBOR

I

SHE felt the burden first in a London market. She said nothing at the time; no one in that party of American tourists suspected her uneasiness, for Jane Addams was not the girl to wince aloud. But the weight on her soul was to grow heavier, until she had to speak at last, as she did to Ellen after the bull fight in Madrid, changing both their lives and the lives of no one knows how many more. . . .

Once in a dream she had felt the same way. She was a frail child of six, then, and lived with her father in a big house among the hills of Cedar Creek, Illinois. The curious vision that came to haunt her night after night was that she alone was alive in all the world. And it seemed to her that the world could be brought back to life by one implement only, a wagon wheel. The pain to her, as she tossed in bed, arose from her burden to build the wheel. She alone was responsible for the fate of the world. . . . The morning after the dream

261

she went to the village blacksmith shop, to study wheelmaking.

"Do you always have to sizzle the iron in water?" she asked the smith.

"Sure, that makes the iron hard."

Jane sighed. Wheelmaking was hard, and Fate had put it into her two small hands.

Such dreams, perhaps, had their roots in her love for her father. Often she had observed him pensive with care, and yearned to help him in his unresting duty. Her father was the leading citizen in his county. He was rich miller, banker, and State Senator. He canvassed for funds to build the railroad, for votes for his friend, Mister Lincoln. Adoring him, his dreamy child wanted to share his numerous cares.

Her father himself always pointed out other people who needed her help. One Sunday, dressing for church, she put on her new coat, and presented herself shyly to her father.

"You look very pretty," he agreed gravely. "But your old coat will be just as warm and won't make other children feel so bad."

The "other children" were those who lived in the back streets of Freeport. She told her father, when he took her through these streets, that she would some day live in a big house. "But it will be right in the midst of horrid little houses like these," she declared.

THE GOOD NEIGHBOR

As she grew older, the child's anxiety for the sorrows of the world was overlaid with happier visions. At Rockford College the young girl, dwelling upon the beauty of the world as it shone from the pages of her books, found peace. But it was a peace from which she was to graduate. Her father died, her fragile health gave way. The doctor prescribed rest and change for her. . . .

And so the pale, tender-eyed girl of twenty-three came to that London market — whereupon the beauty of the world began to fade, and remorse welled up again from the pit of her mind and mixed with the very marrow of her bones.

London to her had meant Westminster Abbey, and William Shakespeare who had written gaily that

> All the world's a stage,
And all the men and women merely players. . . .

and the quaint countryside, and monumental glories of one kind and another. But one Saturday, at midnight, she was taken to the East End. As a tourist, she was told, she would be interested in seeing the Saturday night auction of fruit and vegetables. The bus stopped at the end of a dingy street, and she looked down.

She saw hands; they seemed to her just human hands writhing under the yellow gas flare, like a net haul of fish under the sun. The hands belonged to ragged bodies with pinched faces intent on the rotting vegetable in the huckster's hand.

"A penny, ye beggars," roared the auctioneer.

A man darted from the crowd, a cabbage in his hand. He sat down on the curb, buried his teeth in the raw, unwashed cabbage, and devoured it.

Jane Addams went back to her hotel, steeped in shame. The glories of Westminster Abbey and the Bard of Avon's noble stage faded from her mind. Her quest for Beauty and Truth seemed a childish waste of opportunity. There, in that East End market, were rampant ugliness and lies. They were real.

She kept her distress from her family and friends. They would have said: "Don't be morbid." And the party moved on.

In Germany she recovered her spirits. The sorrows of life were bearable when they filtered grandly through the organ music of Bach and the stained glass of cathedrals. But again a harsh note shattered her harmony. Before breakfast one winter morning in Saxe-Coburg, she looked out of the window of her hotel. Across the town square a single file of women were trooping. Each woman had tied to her back a huge tank filled with hot brew. The women were bent over. Their faces and hands were raw-red from cold, except for white scars.

264

"These scars?" asked Jane Addams.

Burns. The hot stuff splashed when the women stumbled, and so the scars.

She went at once across the square to the brewery. The brewer received her with indifference: men must have beer, and women scars. She went back to the hotel with no appetite for breakfast, no taste for either Gothic architecture or Bach. To mere culture she was becoming as indifferent as the brewer to the scars of his workers. She did not want to visit another cathedral; she wanted to help those women who worked fourteen hours a day for thirty-eight cents.

Yet what did she do about it? She flung the reproachful question at herself. Skinny hands writhed in East London, faces were scarred in Saxe-Coburg — everywhere humanity suffered. She felt its burden of tears, but did nothing to lighten the burden. Instead, she pursued a will-o'-the-wisp of culture, without end, without use.

For four years Jane Addams bore her self-reproach. Then came the crisis in her life, during the Eastertide of 1888. She was again in Europe, this time with her college chum, Ellen Starr. One afternoon, in Madrid, they went to a bullfight. At the death of the first horse in the arena, Ellen left abruptly. Jane stayed to the end, rather enjoying the spectacle. But no sooner did she leave the stands than she was overcome by a feeling of

265

disgust, not for bullfighting, although she thought it brutal, but for herself.

She had looked with indifference upon the murder of a dozen animals. She had no defense against herself, except the excuse of having sought to know the culture of Spain. And that was the excuse of a weakling, she thought bitterly. Her endless drifting in the pools of culture had then brought her to this, that without a qualm she could participate in senseless brutality.

"I have been duped," she thought. "Like many young people, I have gone on and on with my study. Why? For something to do. Something to do! Men are sad, men are lonely, and I have wanted for something to do!"

She said it to Ellen Starr. And she proposed a remedy, for herself and for other young women like herself: —

"Let us," she said, "start a social settlement in America, one like Toynbee Hall in England." Toynbee Hall had been established by philanthropists as a center for helping the London poor. There the poor went for enlightenment or amusement. Young University men mingled with them, instructed them if they wanted instruction, helped them in their problems and in their parties.

Jane Addams had visited Toynbee Hall. "Such a settlement house would be useful in Chicago," she said to Ellen. "Think of all the races in America that have to learn to live together, if our democracy is to endure. At our 'house' we would gather together all sorts of immigrants, do what we could to help them, and give them a life in common."

Ellen was enthusiastic.

"We would not only help them," said Jane Addams frankly. "They would help us. We are smothered in comfort, as they are oppressed by poverty. My scheme is to throw off some of this stifling comfort for the privilege of being of some use in the world."

Ellen kissed her. It was a bargain. And Jane Addams was never so happy. She felt as though she had been absolved from a crime that had lain heavily upon her conscience. All her life, it seems, her conscience had borne the burden — the crime of uselessness. Always she had had a sense of responsibility for the misery around her. Now at last she was about to build the wagon wheel of her dreams. Now, in fact, she was going to live in a big house "right in the midst of horrid little houses."

II

Jane Addams found the "big house" in Chicago, in the shape of an old, run-down mansion built by a man named Hull. Thirty years before,

Mr. Hull had chosen the site for its suburban peace; Jane Addams rented the site for opposite reasons. The Hull House was situated at Halsted and Polk Streets, in the heart of the immigrant quarter of Chicago. The streets and alleys around, dirty and badly lighted, were lined with wooden shanties, many of them without even a water supply save for a faucet in the back yard. Every shanty swarmed with life, human and quadruped. The neighborhood was a study in garbage and children and every language but English. In the very midst of it all stood the once elegant, two-storied brick Hull House; and into it, during September of 1889, with their sofas and rugs, their pictures, books and piano, moved Jane Addams and her friend Ellen Starr.

Their neighbors — Italians, Irish, Greeks, Russian Jews, and Germans — were curious. Why had these two young women, who could afford to live in the better districts of the city — why had they moved right there? When one of the young ladies dropped in to call on the Murphys and the Sicilianos and on others, inviting their young women to dinner and to a "reading party," the neighborhood buzzed with suspicion. There were all sorts of theories to account for the strange behavior of the new folks.

"They'll be wanting to sell you something," said Mr. Murphy.

"Don't promise to go to their church," warned Mr. Siciliano.

"Labor spies!" was perhaps Mr. Stein's theory.

No one suspected an act of pure kindness until the women and children came home with tales of the charm and friendliness of the ladies of Hull House.

"But what did they want you to do?" demanded Suspicion, reluctant to surrender.

"Want? Nothing. Miss Addams is reading a book to us. It's a wonderful story. Imagine! It's by a woman called George — George Eliot. Then we talked about things, mostly about the neighborhood. You know, she's right. She says we ought all to ask for better garbage collection. She thinks so many children die in this neighborhood because the streets are full of garbage all the time."

The women in the rear tenements were more excited when the message reached them that Miss Addams would even mind their children for them. She had begun a nursery for infants and a kindergarten for the little ones, and the mothers who worked out didn't have to lock the children up any longer and worry all day long about their falling out the window.

The neighborhood concluded it was a fine day for them when Miss Addams moved into Hull House.

There seemed to be no limits to her helpfulness. She was equal to anything. She nursed the sick, of course; she wasn't afraid once to prepare a corpse for burial; and another time to be around when a lonely woman had a baby in the middle of the night. Doctors are not easy to reach, especially when you can't pay their fee. Miss Addams helped out with money, too. There was that Italian family, and when the landlord came to put them out, along came Miss Addams with the rent, every cent of it, just as she paid the grocer for that other family.

"Casa di Dio," the Italians called Hull House, and its lady with the tender, gray eyes *"Santa Jane."*

Saintly Jane began her experiment with no clear plan. She knew that first she must understand her poor, bewildered neighbors and their earthly needs, and she must win their friendship. Behind every window of every tenement, life, like a flower, lay withering and rootless. And, good gardener that she was, Jane Addams first studied the human soil in which she was to work.

She came to know the features of every immigrant race, and strove to make Hull House home to each. "These will please my Italians," she might muse as she arranged a vase of roses for the table. "For them, roses are fragrant memories of the old country." Her Italians were sons of

270

the soil. They found hard the crowded, indoor life
of a big city. One Italian woman insisted that Miss
Addams imported her roses from Italy. Poor
woman! It cost five cents to ride to the Park,
and there were no florists near her house. . . .
Her Russian Jews, however, would pass by the
vase of roses as though it came there by mere
chance. Their favorite corner was by the books.
Presently you would hear them, loud in debate.
"They are mighty in debate," thought Jane Addams. For ages they had smarted under the whip
of oppression, and the sense of social justice was
strong in them. . . . Her Greeks, it seemed, preferred the gymnasium to any other part of the
house; although the older Greeks liked to sit and
talk proudly of Homer and Plato. . . . And all
her people had a right to their own talents,
thought Jane Addams, but at Hull House they
could learn to understand one another and their
life in common. Not until they learned that lesson
could they become good citizens in a democracy.

The doors of Hull House were open to everybody. But the deepest concern of Jane Addams
was for the young girls and boys in the streets.
She saw them at work in the factories and shops
of Chicago, twelve hours and more a day. She
beheld in their eyes the bright dreams that per-
fumed the air about them. And at night she saw
them hurry off to claim the promise of those dreams

271

before the factory whistle blew the next morning. In such mood they were prey to all the counterfeit joy of the city, the gin palace, the dance-hall, the lurid movie. Poor, tricked youths! Things did not always turn out well for them, for their anguished mothers often ran to Miss Addams for help: Anna is arrested. Anna is a good girl, and she was going to put back the five dollars she took from the cash box to buy a dress for her church picnic, but her employer found out before she could raise the money, and he wants to send her to prison. . . . Miss Addams, Miss Addams! Mario has been in a fight. A man was killed. Mario didn't mean to do it. And now . . .

Santa Jane's heart ached for those young girls and boys.

Their parents were bewildered. What had happened to their American children? Jane Addams understood. The young people regarded their parents as foreigners. They heard no echoes of their fine past — of Italian art or Hebrew lore — in their parents; they saw only outlandish laborers, and were ashamed. The parents were just as bigoted. They refused to see the youth's craving for change and for power, the daughter's need for a new hat, the son's wanting his own money so that he could "be somebody." The breach between parents and children was wide.

At Hull House Jane Addams sought ways to

draw them together. Her first problem was to attract the young girls and boys of the neighborhood to Hull House. There, through art, music, athletics, and social clubs, they could satisfy their need for excitement and power.

Meanwhile the world at large was hearing of the amazing Jane Addams, and people were peeping in at Hull House: rich men moved to contribute money to Miss Addams' experiment, fashionable young women inspired to help in the good work; and distinguished pilgrims to Chicago's shrine of democracy, Hull House. What they saw sent them away to sing the praises of Jane Addams in all parts of the civilized world. They told perhaps of the Hull House kindergarten; or of a club of children happy over their milk and spaghetti because the teacher was to continue the story of Roland and his knights, after which they could make wooden swords and lances and have a tournament. On that occasion the visitor may have seen the little chap who burst into tears, clapped his cap on, and dashed out, saying: "I ain't comin' back. No use. Roland's dead." The visitor might have told how in the evening every room of Hull House was occupied by a club of adults; here a group discussing labor problems; another studying English poetry; another singing German songs; a sewing class, a cooking class, and so on through the house.

273

The sight-seers came in such numbers that regular guides through Hull House had to serve them, especially when the settlement spread to more buildings. The guides were themselves residents of the settlement, of course, and took pride in conducting the tour.

"That huge building is devoted entirely to our Boys' Club, splendidly equipped with shops, recreation, and study rooms." It is the guide speaking to the tourist. "Over there is our nursery and kindergarten. And that is the Jane Club."

"And what," the tourist may ask, "is the Jane Club?"

Once, during a strike in a local shoe factory, the girl strikers held a meeting at Hull House. They felt that, although justified, they could not hold out against their employer much longer because they had to pay for their board and lodgings.

"Wouldn't it be fine if we had a boarding club of our own!" exclaimed someone. "And then we could stand by each other in a time like this!"

Jane Addams waited for such moments. She promptly read with the young women a book on co-operation. Then they applied the idea to a boarding club. To begin with, Hull House paid the first month's rent on two apartments. Later a clubhouse was built.

"And that," says the guide, "is the Jane Club,

founded and run by women, the first of its kind in America. . . . Here is our Art Gallery, where our people may study painting."

"What do the poor want with art?" the tourist may be permitted to inquire. To which the astonishing answer is that the Art Gallery is one of the most popular adjuncts of the whole settlement.

The party comes to the Hull House Labor Museum, which also has an interesting story. . . . Jane Addams, meditating upon the breach between American children and their immigrant parents, feared that Old-World family life was breaking down in the New World. "There ought to be some way of bridging the gap between the old and the new generation," she felt.

One day, walking down Polk Street, she came upon an old Italian woman sitting in the sun on the steps of a tenement house, spinning thread with a simple stick spindle. The old woman might have served as a model for one of Michelangelo's Fates, but that is not why she arrested the attention of Jane Addams.

"Here is the bridge between the old and the new," thought Jane Addams. "The children of this old Italian work in factories with complicated machines. But just as they are descended from the old woman, their complicated machines are descended from her simple one. This the children do not realize. If we but made them feel it, they

275

would be more sympathetic to their elders. They would see the link between the past and present, between themselves and their parents."

She ransacked the neighborhood for spinning wheels and old weaver's frames, and put them all on display in Hull House. The following Saturday evening she called the neighbors in for a party. Among others were present a Syrian woman, a Greek, an Italian, a Russian, and an Irishwoman. All of them were adepts at the spinning wheel, and felt bound by a common Fate despite their differences of race. The young people looked on in pleased wonderment while their parents performed. One young Italian girl, who had been ashamed to accompany her mother to Hull House because of "the old lady's" head-kerchief and homespun garments, suddenly found this same mother the center of admiration.

"Is it true," she asked Miss Addams, "that my mother is the best stick-spindle spinner in America?"

Jane Addams smiled. She mentioned casually the lovely Italian village in which the girl's mother had spent her youth, how she had come by her skill, how right she was not to give up the fine head-kerchief for an ugly store hat, how hard it was for her to be torn away from her old home and made to give up everything — even her talents — to become a stranger in America.

276

That was the beginning of the Labor Museum, where immigrants came to exercise their craft in pottery, metal, and wood. It helped to bring children and parents closer together, and men of different races. Perhaps the Labor Museum, as a school of democracy, was Jane Addams's most brilliant idea.

The tourist to Hull House always wanted to be taken to the one in whose heart Hull House was first built, perhaps to touch her hand and say grateful things to her, and hear her murmur:

"Very kind of you, I'm sure. I hardly deserve all that."

She could always be found in the settlement; that is, unless she was at some neighbor's. For whenever trouble arose, at once an appeal was sent to Miss Addams. Did the collector come to take away Pasquale's furniture? Were the officers taking Mrs. Murphy to the poor house, and she, poor soul, fighting the officers? Miss Addams protected them all. In her their faith reposed as in their Lady All-Beneficent. Once a young man who in the heat of a dispute had killed another fled, in his panic, to her. A few minutes later, the frantic brother of the murdered man rushed in.

She failed no one who came in need. One night, a busy burglar stepped into the second story of Hull House. He found himself in a bedroom. His dark lantern played contemplatively around. Suddenly he heard a famous, girlish voice say: "Don't make a noise, people are asleep." The burglar leaped for the window. "You'll be hurt if you go that way," the voice said. "Go down by the stairs and let yourself out." A moment later the man tiptoed sheepishly out the front door. A second burglar, interrupted in his nightwork at Hull House, was so panicky that Miss Addams decided he was a novice. "Come back at nine in the morning," she said. "I'll see what I can do about getting you a job." He came, and the underworld lost an apprentice.

There are public champions celebrated for their service in one cause or another: the welfare of children, of labor, of a downtrodden race. Some raise the banner of free speech, of free schools, of justice here or there. Jane Addams embraced all causes for the welfare of one race — the human. She was the very symbol of America, a refuge and an opportunity, where children and parents, one race and another, one class and another, lived together on the common ground of forbearance and sympathy.

After the bullfight, when she escaped from the ivory tower of No Purpose in which she had found herself locked, she began her new life simply by moving into an old house at Halsted and Polk Streets, Chicago, and calling on her neighbors.

Sometimes she could help them without having to leave the vicinity, as with the nursery and the Labor Museum. But often the hurt of her people had its roots far off in the legal chambers of the city or nation. On those occasions, Jane Addams put on her hat and coat, so to speak, and went forth from Hull House.

III

"Your American Presidents come and go, and we in England often do not remember their names, but we all know Jane Addams, and can never forget her." So said a prominent English speaker.

"No, I never heard of Lake Michigan or the Chicago stockyards," admitted an Australian visitor in public interview. "But there is a hospital ward in Sydney which is dedicated to Jane Addams. Is she really the only woman in America? She is the only one our papers quote."

One of the Chicago newspapers once asked editorially: "Who are the first five citizens of Chicago? Of course there can be no doubt of the first — Jane Addams leads all."

Settlements were springing up throughout the country, all modeled after that of Jane Addams. Hull House itself now occupied a group of structures covering a city block. And its founder's reputation covered the globe.

From thousands of platforms people heard her speak, and the books she wrote reached millions who had not the pleasure of hearing her. Her word carried such weight that political leaders, not only of her own but of other countries, sought her advice and support. To everyone she made audible the cry of children and the weariness of workers. She showed the waste of good human stuff in our industrial life. She made known the trials of motherhood, and other feminine problems which led her into the van of the fight begun in Susan Anthony's day, for woman's rights. But her two chief crusades were on behalf of children and World Peace.

The youth of twenty nationalities came to Hull House. To them Jane Addams was neither saint nor world celebrity. She was their friend who loved them, good or wicked. If little Mary was beaten by her drunken father, she came sobbing to Miss Addams. If Tony broke a window with his ball, he neither ran away nor lied; he brought the matter to Miss Addams. Hull House, after school hours, belonged to children, every room of it. At school, the pupils did only what teacher wanted, but in Hull House they did what they themselves wanted. They were free to join in the activity of the music group or the dancing group, the theater group, the artists. Many a youth found his future career in Hull House, where he first let loose his dreams.

Shortly after Hull House had started a man came to see Miss Addams. He had sat among an audience she addressed the evening before, he said. Her words had made him feel rather uncomfortable, touched his conscience, in fact. He was a rich man, perhaps a selfish one. What, now, could he do?

Jane Addams knew of her visitor. Referring to a block of ramshackle houses owned by him, she said: "They are unfit to live in. You might tear them down and build a playground. Our children have no outdoor life but in the streets." And that remark of hers was the origin of the playground system of Chicago.

It was one thing, however, to build facilities for the happiness of children, and quite another to release the many of them from their grinding labor.

"Do have some candy," Jane Addams had urged the little girls who came to the first Christmas party at Hull House. "No, thank you, Ma'am." They worked fourteen hours a day in a candy factory. Candy had no attraction for them.

Jane Addams had seen children five years old pulling out basting-thread from the garments their mothers sewed at home, mother and child earning

281

together about ten cents an hour. She knew of a boy killed and two others badly hurt tending a machine in a factory near Hull House.

"Our efforts for our children are hopeless," said Jane Addams to her associates at Hull House, "unless we abolish child labor. And we can do that only by piercing the conscience of the people with the ugly facts of child labor."

Hull House went out after the facts; Miss Jane Addams became America's leading authority on the national disease of child labor. She spent a dozen years speaking and writing on the subject. She enlisted the forces of labor and religion in the crusade. Advocating a bill against child labor, she went before legislatures and governors. At last, in 1903, her campaign was crowned with victory, when the bill she fought for became the law of Illinois.

In the campaign, moreover, she found herself shoulder to shoulder with all organized workers in their struggle for a fair wage and enough leisure. In Hull House, the women cloak and shirt makers of Chicago formed their first union.

"Workers have the right to unite," she declared. But she shrank from strife in any form; and fair-minded employers and workers, knowing that she had at heart the welfare of all, trusted her to arbitrate their disputes.

Her second crusade for the common good was

against war. Not the price of war, nor even the horror of it, moved her most to mobilize public opinion against it. The most deplorable effect of war was, to the founder of Hull House, that it destroyed the bonds of sympathy among people. Those bonds, for her, were the paramount beauty of life, and Hull House was a seedbed for their bloom. She knew how microscopic the germ that too often checked their flowering. She recalled Pasquale, the lad who refused to sit alongside Angelina when he first came to Hull House.

"She," he said contemptuously, "eat her macaroni like *that*. But we," — he demonstrated with pride, — "we eat it like *this*."

At Hull House Pasquale learned not to judge by his own code of table manners, but by another code common to Angelina and him both.

"When, say, a South Italian Catholic is forced to make friends with an Austrian Jew," Jane Addams believed, "he gradually loses his prejudice against both Jews and Austrians." Thus America, home of all races, dissolves all racial prejudice.

Her efforts in the cause of peace were lifelong. She lectured widely on it; she wrote a book which became popular, called "The Newer Ideals of Peace"; she became the head of the American Women's Peace Party. Finally, in February of 1915, women from the war-racked countries of Europe sent an appeal to her to join them at The

283

Hague, where several months later she founded the Women's International League for Peace and Freedom.

In 1931 she was awarded the Nobel Peace Prize.

"In Jane Addams," said the speaker presenting the prize, "there are assembled all the best womanly attributes which shall help us to establish peace in the world.

"She has taught tolerance and peaceful community living, first at home and then in the world at large." So ran the screed of another of her prizes, the American Education Award, the same year she died.

Homage to her was world-wide, and offered from high places. But as an expression of the simple gratitude of humanity, she would have liked best to hear what an old Greek murmured on his knees beside her coffin: —

"Her no just one people, her no just one religion. Her all peoples, all religions."

12

The New Freedom

WOODROW WILSON

At last a President of the United States proclaimed to all the world that his country's ideals were those of humanity anywhere, at any time. He did more. He made plans to rebuild the tottering world in accordance with those ideals. But first he renewed them in the American structure where they had somewhat decayed. WOODROW WILSON'S story is one of the noblest in history.

THE NEW FREEDOM

I

IN the last days of the year 1918, when the smoke of the Great War rolled away, the surviving world turned its agonized eyes to one man of all men. For more than four years mankind, tricked by its leaders, had been driven to die in the trenches of Europe; and the hearts of the living had died in the ruins about them. Then it was, above the mists of poison gas, they heard his voice. With healing fire his words touched each sufferer. He spoke of peace, of the dawn of a new day in which peace was everlasting. He spoke not for a nation but for humanity. On every torn soul he laid the quickening poultice of hope and his resolve: —

"This agony must not be gone through with again."

When the news broke following the Armistice that this man had arrived in Europe, the distressed from every quarter of the world strove to reach him. Him alone they trusted, victor and vanquished alike. Crowds pressed around his carriage to be

287

refreshed by a glimpse of their prophet. Ador-
ingly, blindly, they followed him about, as though
to be healed of woe by his touch. In Paris, where
he came to lay out his blueprint for a better
world, all manner of men waited upon him: Mos-
lems in turbans, gaberdined Jews from the ghettos
of Eastern Europe, black men with rings in their
ears, and sober Europeans with portfolios filled
with hope.

The power of the prophet was without parallel
in history. The world was a sphere spinning to the
gravity of his thought, its people his faithful.
Physically he was a frail man. He stood a little
above the average height. His eyes were large,
his face smooth and gaunt. His head and face were
granite gray, cut fine. Perhaps his most character-
istic features were the granite jaw, the rigid
mouth, and the fixed, aloof eyes.

Such was Woodrow Wilson, President of the
United States.

II

Only nine years before his own neighbors had
been hardly aware of him.

"Who is this Wilson?" asked the Democratic
party boss of New Jersey.

The question was important just then. The Democratic party chief had got a "tip." It was: Run

Professor Wilson for Governor. The politicians scratched their heads.

"A dumb idea!" they believed at first. "This man's never been in politics before. Who knows him? What's he done?"

They consulted further. They could not afford to leave any possibility unprobed. The public was restless, not only in New Jersey but throughout the nation. In the next campaign, the old political claptrap would not do. The times were in ferment. Dissatisfied with his share in the wealth and management of the country, the voter was ready for a new kind of leader. The "boss" felt his old supports creaking under him. He could save himself only by repairing his structure with new planks and a new face upon them. The Democratic boss of New Jersey was shrewd enough to "size up" the situation, and listened patiently to the advice of running for Governor a candidate with no political experience.

"What's this Wilson done?" he asked.

Woodrow Wilson, professor at Princeton and president of the university, was at that moment attracting wide attention. He had not intended it. He had intended only to improve life on the campus. He had no idea, when he began, that the trouble would overrun the bounds of the campus. He was startled when it embroiled the whole State of New Jersey. Later he discovered that the roots of the trouble underspread the nation. And finally, the fight he began for the reform of life at Princeton University ended in his monumental effort for the whole human race.

The trouble began with the sophomores. When a Princetonian became a sophomore, he also became a clubman, or rather he became eligible for the membership of some one of the group of clubs on the campus. These clubs, rivaling one another in splendor and exclusiveness, awoke in the sophomore breast curious ambitions: Oh, to wear the hatband of the "Ivy" or the "Tiger Inn," or even the "Colonial." Spring was the critical season for the sophomore; then he knew the bliss of the elect or the despair of the damned. Up to then he hung suspended in limbo. He weighed his chances: How "good" was his family? How rich his father? Meanwhile his studies had little to do with his career at Princeton. For half of Princeton they were details against a bright background of club life.

As head of the University, Woodrow Wilson thought the clubs harmful, and proposed to abolish them. He put it, at first, lightly: —

"The side shows are swallowing up the circus. Moreover, I won't be president of a country club," he said.

The rich alumni protested. "Abolish the clubs and Old Nassau can never be the same."

Rich parents protested: "Must our sons associate with muckers, and not with those of their own class as they may in their clubs?"

Woodrow Wilson was astonished, like a man who in trying to repair a leak brings down a storm upon himself. "The clubs are undemocratic," he pointed out. "They are contrary to the principles of our country."

His opponents were powerful, and club life went gaily on. Deciding that more was at stake than hatbands, snobs, or sophomores, Woodrow Wilson carried his appeal outside Princeton. In print and on platform he crusaded. "The wealthy seek to control our colleges," he declared. "They prevent us from serving the people. The universities would make men forget their common origins and join a class — and no class ever can serve America."

With this thought he diverted a college family quarrel into the troubled tide of national affairs. Two things about his crusade served to arrest the attention of the public at large. First, there was then widespread but scattered opinion that the whole nation was suffering from a decay of democracy and abuse of wealth. Woodrow Wilson's fight against these evils in Princeton established him as the spokesman for this scattered sentiment. But more remarkable was the hypnotic power and lift of the professor's speech. He had a way of making one squirm or cheer.

Bankers squirmed and sneered: "Schoolmaster." Woodrow Wilson bowed to the compliment and went on instructing his growing class of admirers.

Thoughtful patriots cheered and rallied to his words as to a banner. "Here is a man for our White House," they said.

Politicians, their wet fingers up to the wind of public opinion, charted their course accordingly. "The professor might be useful," the New Jersey "boss" admitted. "He makes good speeches, and the public trusts him. He is no politician, but that may be in his favor: the public is to-day impatient with politicians. If there is nothing discreditable in his past, we can sound him out."

His past was spotless. As a child he was Tommy Wilson: Thomas Woodrow Wilson, son of a Southern preacher. In Staunton, Virginia, there still stands the fine house in which he was born on December 28, 1856. His family did not stay in Staunton. When he became conscious of his surroundings, he found himself living in Augusta, Georgia. There Tommy dreamed away the years that shaped him into a handsome but frail, spectacled boy. However delicate his health, though, he often escaped in spirited adventures. He fought valiantly, he hunted treasures. Frequently he boarded his good ship the *Avenger* and chased pirates all through the South Seas. Sitting against a tree in the pine woods, his nose in a book, he had all those adventures. When his family moved to Wilmington, North Carolina, Tommy yearned so for a real *Avenger* and real pirates that he sometimes shut his book and walked down to the harbor to talk with the sailors. Once he came near running away to sea. What deterred him, perhaps, was that he could not take all his books with him. And without books to read or to talk about, life even on the *Avenger* would be dull.

In due time the boy tramping with a book through the Southern pine woods became the student at Princeton College. The *Avenger* still lived in his mind, but now it had turned into the American Ship of State; Tom Wilson, by the light of the midnight oil, delighted to cruise in American history. Pirates there still were for him, but changed into the form of High Tariffs and Pork Barrels and suchlike public menaces. As for chasing these pirates, Tom Wilson did that ably, *pro* and *con,* in the debating society. His chief interest was history and politics, his chief activity debating.

"I'll argue that with you when I meet you in the Senate some day," he used to say.

While still at college he wrote an article on politics which was published in a well-known magazine. It was a proud day for him when he got his first author's check, and he contemplated a long career of similar checks. As the name Thomas W. Wilson rose imperishably on the printed page, it struck him that an author ought to have a more distinctive trade mark.

"Let's see now," he mused. "How would Thomas Wilson do? T. Woodrow Wilson, perhaps. Ah — Woodrow Wilson."

It was still Tom Wilson, however, who graduated from Princeton in 1879 and enrolled in the law school of the University of Virginia. At the end of the first year his poor body broke down under the pace of his mind, and he was forced to continue his study of the law at home. In 1882 he opened an office in Atlanta, ostensibly for the practice of law. But if a client ever wandered into the office he found Woodrow Wilson, Esquire, too busy to take a case. He was writing the first of his many books, "Congressional Government in the United States." No, despite his skill as a debater, Woodrow Wilson was ill-suited to the law. A scholar's robe was to him more becoming. He closed his office and entered Johns Hopkins University, from which he emerged several years later: Woodrow Wilson, Ph.D.

Ten years after he left Princeton as a student he returned to it as a professor of Political Science. The students saw him as a slender, handsome man with dreamy eyes and a gentle voice, whose lectures were too good to "cut." But even more admirable than his expertness as scholar and writer was the spirit in which he presented the ideals of America. Four times the students voted him the most popular man on the faculty. The trustees, who had never before been unanimous in anything, in 1902 elected him unanimously President of Princeton. . . .

Everyone knew the rest: how Woodrow Wilson at once began to reform the institution until he had raised it to its place with the greatest universities of the world; how a new enthusiasm seemed to permeate the college and filter down even to the last freshman, who began to study a little harder; how now, in 1910, he wanted to destroy the aristocratic clubs and class distinctions on the campus, for these offended all his American ideals.

The more the Democratic Party boss of New Jersey thought about Woodrow Wilson, the more enthusiastic he waxed. The tip was a good one. With the Professor for a front, the Democrats might again ride into control. He would see the Professor.

III

Three years went by.

When the sun broke through the clouds over Washington on March 4, 1913, it shone down on marching troops and flying colors. A little past one o'clock the vast crowd on the plaza of the Capitol broke into wild cheering. On the platform were the judges of the Supreme Court, the Congress, and the Diplomatic Corps of the United States. But the cheering was meant for the spare, gaunt figure in the rostrum. The man who had recently stepped out of a cloister of books was about to take the inaugural oath of the President of the United States.

The police kept forcing the crowds back, to leave free the space around the rostrum.

"Let the people come forward," ordered the President-elect.

When the people had gathered about him he leaned forward and began: —

"My fellow citizens, there has been a change of government. What does the change mean?"

He spoke clearly, easily, and the men and women in the street heard him in deep silence. He spoke of the wealth of American life, the beauty and strength of it.

"But the evil has come with the good," he said with passion. "We have been proud of our industrial achievements, but we have not hitherto stopped thoughtfully enough to count the human cost . . . to the men and women and children upon whom the dead weight and burden of it all has fallen pitilessly the years through. The groan-

296

ing and agony of it all . . . coming up out of the mines and factories. . . ."

This was the strain that had sent the many voters to mark the ballot as they did. He went on, still harking back:

"The great Government we loved has too often been made use of for private and selfish purposes, and those who used it had forgotten the people. Our thought has been 'Let every man look out for himself, let every generation look out for itself.' "

His voice rose, the tone of it more hopeful. To the upturned eyes of the multitude he brought a vision of the future. Yes, our industry and wealth were great; but our first thought must be to shield our men and women from being crushed by so much wealth. He foretold laws and measures whose purpose was to provide a larger share of happiness for the man underneath the wheel of industry.

"This is not a day of triumph; it is a day of dedication," he solemnly closed. "Men's hearts wait upon us; men's lives hang in the balance; men's hopes call upon us. . . . I summon all honest men, all patriotic, all forward-looking men, to my side."

The throaty roar, as he stepped down, swept the country. Here was the leader long awaited by the people; the hour and its man were both theirs. The professional politicians gaped. The schoolmaster held in his thin fist the will of the nation, caught by the magic of words. Only three years before he had been ready to retire into the obscure peace of a cottage and end his days writing his books, to live for his country only as a name on the shelves of a library. Now his words had taken wing and lifted him to the most conspicuous post in the country.

"Campaign stuff," had sneered the politicians when he toured New Jersey as a candidate for Governor. He was denouncing "boss" rule.

"In the interest of the people I go to the Governor's chair," he had said publicly. "If the Democratic Party does not understand that, it ought not elect me."

The election in New Jersey had been a "landslide" for Woodrow Wilson. The country had watched. Would he redeem his campaign pledges?

One day the political boss came to see the newly-elected Governor. He was thinking, he said, of "going" to the Senate. The Governor was frank in replying that he would oppose him. The boss was shocked. He was also incredulous. Some things a mere Governor did not dare. He then proceeded with his plans — and made his last political blunder. Woodrow Wilson did what later he was often to do: he went to the people, and the people responded to his appeal for honest politics by unbossing the boss.

THE NEW FREEDOM

"He's a terrible man to manage," said the politicians disgustedly.

What a fighter was this thin scholarly man! Honest people everywhere enjoyed the spectacle of the innocent schoolmaster beating the "gang." But they enjoyed most the schoolmaster's style of fighting: He won by arousing ideals in the hearts of people. They were the eternal ideals of justice and mercy, and the well-known ideals of the Declaration of Independence, but Woodrow Wilson had the uncanny power of rousing them to the day's task.

The fight against the politicians in New Jersey led to a more serious one. Back of the politicians were huge business corporations. Their lawyers drew many a bill for the Legislature, so many that New Jersey was known contemptuously as the "mother of trusts." Such was the state of corruption when Woodrow Wilson walked into the Legislature, and frightened the corporation lawyers out of their wits. "The Governor is an executive," they protested. "He has no right in the Legislature."

But Woodrow Wilson remained the people's advocate. The result was that New Jersey gave up her nurture of trusts, and became one of the most advanced of state governments. When a cheer went up over the country for Woodrow Wilson, he was amazed that merely doing one's duty should

299

cause such excitement. It was not only his doing his duty, however, that brought forth the cheer; it was mainly his vision of duty. Spiritually he was an heir of Thomas Jefferson.

"The aim of the government," he believed, "is to promote the freedom of its people."

He tried to apply this principle at Princeton. As Governor of New Jersey he tried to apply it to the state. And in 1912 the people sent him to the White House to apply it to the whole country.

He had no sooner delivered his inaugural address than he began nothing short of a peaceful revolution. The time was ripe.

"Democracy is passing," lamented many thoughtful Americans. "For twenty years the frontier has been no more. Without a frontier, the pioneer spirit dies out and with it the spirit of freedom. The free, open space has become the city and the slum. The spirited pioneers have become beggars and wage-slaves. And instead of a government by the people, we have a government by bankers and magnates."

But Woodrow Wilson proclaimed his faith in a New Democracy, a New Freedom, to replace the older pioneer democracy. No longer do we have a frontier, he admitted; but we still have its ideals. Once the frontier alone was shield against the oppression of the powerful; now the people's government must forge the shield. Then democracy would have a new birth.

To hasten the advent of the New Democracy he sought the advice of those he called "forward-looking men." He appointed to his cabinet a labor leader. Samuel Gompers, too, was frequently at the White House. As Assistant Secretary of Labor he chose a follower of Henry George. He consulted with Charles W. Eliot of Harvard. Then he led Congress in some of the greatest achievements of its career. There are formal names for those remarkable Acts: the Federal Reserve, Rural Credits, the Federal Trade Commission, the Clayton Anti-Trust Act, the Adamson Act. All of them expressed Woodrow Wilson's vision of justice and better life for the worker, the farmer, the small businessman. And from that vision he would not take his eyes.

Conservative people began to wince at the pace at which he was leading them forward. But he did not slacken: "God knows," he said, "there are enough things in this world that need to be corrected."

"How are we to give the American people," he put the problem, "and, by example, the people of the world, more liberty, more happiness, more prosperity; and make prosperity a common heritage instead of a selfish possession?"

"The people of the world." Woodrow Wilson's

vision expanded boldly. Once he sought to perfect democracy in Princeton, later throughout the state, now throughout the nation, and soon for all the world. America would not become smug and selfish, he hoped, like a rich man who is callous to the suffering of his neighbors.

IV

Beyond the borders of the United States the world began to seethe like a volcano. The first eruption came from across the Rio Grande, where a revolution broke out. Now the magnates of the United States, as well as those of England and Germany, had been using the soil of Mexico for their own tillage, and they foresaw their rich yield imperiled. Indignantly they appealed to the White House.

"Order!" they cried. "We must have order in Mexico. Let the President protect our citizens in Mexico. Where is our Army, our Navy?"

But President Wilson was cold to the entreaty. Professor Wilson, the historian, knew that the spirit of liberty was now over Mexico, inspiring the peons to regain the land of which they had been robbed.

Order, yes. "But no one asks for order," he said sharply, "because order will help the masses of

302

people. All demand it so that the great owners of property, the men who have exploited that rich country for their own selfish purposes, shall be able to continue."

A golden opportunity came to the magnates through the stupid discourtesy of a Mexican officer toward some American soldiers. "War on Mexico!" they yelled. "We have been insulted."

It would have been, as it once was, a simple affair for the "Giant of the North" to crush Mexico — simple, and profitable to the magnates with stakes there. President Wilson did not act for them. He rather kept in mind the misery of the peons.

"My passion is for the submerged eighty-five per cent. of the people of Mexico who are now struggling for liberty," he said. His country, he declared, was devoted to the spirit of liberty anywhere in the world. It was no conquering nation. It would not hinder the rise of any people to the invigorating heights of democracy.

The people of Latin America sat up and rubbed their eyes. Had the Giant of the North really put aside his club and picked up an olive branch? Was it to them, to such weaklings as Nicaragua and San Domingo and Colombia, that he extended it? They watched suspiciously.

"But the Mexicans are not fit to govern themselves," said the foreign tillers of Mexican wealth.

"No people, properly directed, are not fitted for self-government," replied Woodrow Wilson.

One by one he convinced the neighbors of the United States of his sincerity, of his passion for the welfare of their people, of his wish to deal with them on no other than moral grounds.

"Morality is all right," remarked Kaiser Wilhelm II cynically, "but what about dividends?"

Woodrow Wilson was not cynical. May their revolution bring the peons liberty, he prayed. Remembering his own nation's struggle for it, he would not interfere in Mexico's. Yet he did interfere. Was he wrong to do so? He had said he wouldn't. Was he, too, a hypocrite with lofty talk about friendship for the Mexican people? Well, it was because he was no hypocrite, because his passion for democracy was real, that he interfered. A dictator had sprung up in Mexico. Woodrow Wilson could be calm and diplomatic in all questions except those involving human freedom. And the ideal of peace he put above all others except the ideal of democracy. On this account he interfered in Mexico. And he drove the dictator out.

Standing before the graduates at Annapolis in June 1914, Commander in Chief Woodrow Wilson defined their duty. As sailors they would cruise in all parts of the earth. "You are champions of your fellow men," he said. "Come back and tell us where you see men suffering. Tell us

what service the United States can render. Her
flag is the flag not only of America, but of humanity."

Two months later the flames of the World War
broke out.

At first Woodrow Wilson was stunned. Such
things could not happen. The world was too civilized. This was the work of a few madmen. . . .
But the flames and the madness spread.

When the first shock to him passed, he said
to his fellow countrymen: Here is our chance. We
are the only strong nation at peace. Since we are
made up of all nationalities, we want to speak for
all. If we remain calm, we can perhaps save the
world. Let us be neutral. . . . So he spoke because the heat and the madness were in the atmosphere.

To the clamor of the war chiefs he was cold.
He thought of the war from the standpoint of the
plain man, the man "killed in action" for he knew
not what, the woman limply holding the official
notice of condolence. And he heard them say:
"God, no war." Clearer than ever, he saw the
world in which that man and woman lived, a world
so constituted that even in peace they were in the
paralyzing grip of war. Large standing armies and
navies battened upon them. The small nations
were prey to the big. By force of arms the powerful states of Europe had taken over peoples alien

to themselves and made them bitter by oppression. It was a world steeped in hatred and fear, exploding naturally in recurrent war.

"Is there no hope then of a better life for humanity?" The question lived with Woodrow Wilson, sat down to the table with him, rose in the morning with him. He had appealed to the chiefs of the warring nations. But they had acted like squabbling children who point fingers at each other — "He did it" — and keep on; and they kept on printing stacks of official condolences. . . . There was but one answer to the question, thought Woodrow Wilson: The world must be rebuilt.

When he considered the plan for a new world, a world without war, Professor Wilson recalled the problem of the Thirteen American States, back in 1787. Each one of them had different interests. They might have gone their separate ways, and in time raised grudges and armies. New York might have gobbled up New Jersey. Massachusetts and Connecticut, fearing New York, would perhaps have formed an alliance with Pennsylvania. And so on to endless wars. What saved the colonies was their union in the spirit of democracy. The cure of war was democracy.

In the new world rising from the ashes of this one, thought Woodrow Wilson, democracy must be universal. If the war brought forth such a

306

world, it was a war worth while, and to die in it
glorious.

As in the days at Princeton when he sought to
rebuild the college on democratic lines, and afterward as a candidate for public office preaching
the New Democracy, Woodrow Wilson spoke to the
people of his ideal. Now his message was to the
whole world. The master had taken humanity at
large for his pupil.

Meanwhile the flames began to lick the shores
of America. President Wilson tried heroically to
keep his country "the only great nation at peace."
But he discovered that the whole world structure,
America included, was built of inflammable stuff.
Those days and nights leading up to April, 1917
were tragic for the frail man in the White House.
His suffering soul was in his eyes, in the ghastly
pallor of his face. But his mouth was hard.

He called his advisers to him. He was going to
ask Congress for war, he said. He could see no
loophole of escape.

"What else can I do?"

Nothing, they said. He had done all that was
humanly possible.

"Yes, but do you realize what that means?" he
brooded. America, like the rest, would go war-
mad. For a time, Democracy would die in America. It meant that Germany would be badly
crushed; that the victorious Allies would be mad

enough to insist on a peace that would keep her crushed. It meant, Woodrow Wilson foresaw, that he himself would fail. Not at first. He would be idolized at first, and then attacked. But he had no choice. He must lead his fellow-countrymen into war.

Now above the roar and the madness, the voice of Woodrow Wilson resounded in the ears of the world. He spoke frequently in those days, too frequently for his health. And he spoke for the whole world, he alone. No one else spoke for the German and the Frenchman both. Perhaps no one else would have been believed had he said: "We look for no profit."

"The President" surpassed himself as a magician with words. His thought was clothed in a kind of sunlit beauty, and brought a healing touch. "We are fighting for what we believe and wish to be the rights of mankind," he convinced one. His words may have counted more than the deeds of generals. Above the trenches they flared up in a blaze of ideals, and lit up a vision in the hearts of the dying men. About to throw a grenade, the enemy soldier might have felt the tug on his arm of Woodrow Wilson's assurance: "We have no quarrel with the German people."

The President said that the people of one nation have no quarrel with the people of any other nation. He spoke for every man about to die in battle, for every woman about to be widowed. War was brought on, then, by a few autocrats. The present war was waged to free the German people themselves from their autocratic rulers. On July 4, 1918, he boldly called upon them to revolt against their rulers. Four months later the Kaiser was driven out of Germany. Democracy took another nation into her fold.

Victory, cried the Allies.

No, said Woodrow Wilson; Peace, not victory. "Peace without victory," was his watchword; everlasting peace built on the principle that governments are the servants of their people, and guaranteed by a league of such governments against war. This was the thought in his famous program of Fourteen Points, and to it the stricken people of the world responded as to the holy words of a savior. When the guns were at last silent, Woodrow Wilson was the world's only hope.

On December 2, 1918, he stood before Congress to say that he was wanted at the Peace Table in Europe. "I go to give the best that is in me. . . . I shall make my absence as brief as possible, and shall hope to return with the happy assurance that it has been possible to translate into action the great ideals for which America has striven."

He was carrying to the world the American ideals of permanent peace and democracy. Only for these, he felt, the dead had not died in vain.

The story is not yet finished. It goes on to tell how Woodrow Wilson's sad prophecy came true: how he found himself lonely at the Peace Table; how, once he had saved them, the victorious leaders laughed at his terms of "Peace without victory," and demanded the savage peace of conquerors; how they defeated the hopes of the people thereby; how his own country would not join the League of Nations he had founded; and how he died overtaxing his strength with appeals to the people, to whom he always went for sustenance.

And is the story of Woodrow Wilson at last finished?

Was his passion for world democracy vain?